Sylvia Plath:

The Bell Jar and Poems

"rb wire snare" (26); "Dachau, Auschwitz, Belsen," sites o
r II C — death camps (33); "Luftwaffe," the German ai

∞Writers and Their Works∞

Sylvia Plath:
The Bell Jar and Poems

Raychel Haugrud Reiff

Marshall Cavendish
Benchmark
New York

With special thanks to Diane Middlebrook, professor of English, emerita, Stanford University, for her expert review of this manuscript.

Marshall Cavendish Benchmark
99 White Plains Road
Tarrytown, NY 10591
www.marshallcavendish.us

All Internet sites were available and accurate when sent to press.

All quotations are cited in the text. Additional information and sources are included in the Notes section of this book.

Library of Congress Cataloging-in-Publication Data

Reiff, Raychel Haugrud.
Sylvia Plath : The bell jar and poems / by Raychel Haugrud Reiff.
p. cm. — (Writers and their works)
Includes bibliographical references and index.
Summary: "A biography of writer Sylvia Plath that describes her era, her major works—the novel The bell jar and her poetry—her life, and the legacy of her writing"—Provided by publisher.
ISBN 978-0-7614-2962-3
1. Plath, Sylvia. 2. Poets, American—20th century—Biography. I. Title.
PS3566.L27Z845 2008
811'.54—dc22
[B]

2007035669

Photo research by Lindsay Aveilhe and Linda Sykes/Linda Sykes Photo Research, Hilton Head, SC

AP/Wide World Photos: cover, 2; Bettmann/Corbis: 8, 35, 56, 59, 61; Mortimer Rare Book Room, Smith College, Estate of Aurelia Greenwood Schober: 11, 13; Courtesy Condé Nast Publications: 18; The Granger Collection: 24, 52, 80; Mortimer Rare Book Room, Smith College, Estate of Ted Hughes: 28; The Lilly Library, Indiana University: 30; Ted Hughes Collection, The Woodruff Library, Emory University: 38; John Howard/Cordaly Photo Ltd./Corbis: 46; Cover from *The Bell Jar* by Sylvia Plath. Copyright 1966 Faber and Faber Ltd., London, UK Reprinted by permission of Faber and Faber: 62; H. Armstrong Roberts/Corbis: 67; National Geographic/Getty Images: 79; Cover from *Ariel* by Sylvia Plath. Copyright 1966 Harper & Row, New York. Reprinted by permission of Harper Collins: 90; Musée Bonnet, Bayonne, France/Réunion des Musées Nationaux/Art Resource, NY: 102; BBC/Zuma/Corbis: 112; Cover from *Letters Home* by Sylvia Plath. Copyright 1975 Harper & Row, New York. Reprinted by permission of Harper Collins: 117.

Publisher: Michelle Bisson
Art Director: Anahid Hamparian
Series design by Sonia Chaghatzbanian

Printed in Malaysia
1 3 5 6 4 2

Contents

Introduction   7

Chapter 1.   The Life of Sylvia Plath   9

Chapter 2.   Sylvia Plath's Times   53

Chapter 3.   *The Bell Jar*   63

Chapter 4.   Poetry   91

Chapter 5.   Plath's Place in Literature   113

Works   119

Filmography   120

Chronology   121

Notes   125

Further Information   132

Bibliography   133

Index   141

y is full of in Nazi/Jewish imagery. German tongue
b wire snare" (28); "Dachau, Auschwitz, Belsen," sites of W
II German death camps (33); "Luftwaffe," the German air
orld War II (42); "neat mustache," a reminder of Hitler
an eye, bright blue," a reference to the Nazi's idea tha
d, blue-eyed Aryan race was superior to others (44); "Pan
an for armored tank (45); "swastika" (46); "Fascist" (48);
kampf," the title of Adolf Hitler's autobiography and p
manifesto which in translation means "My Struggle"
e allusions depict the father as an evil, domineer
eling man, a "brute" (49, 50). They also show the victim
tormentors as part of worldwide problems and situat
n incorporates two additional images, the devil and a
to show the evils of domination; in particular, the
ed by a patriarchal society that marginalizes women. "De

ll of in Nazi/Jewish imagery: "German tongue" (16); "Barb
e" (26); "Dachau, Auschwitz, Belsen," sites of World Wa
an death camps (33); "Luftwaffe," the German air forc
l War II (42); "neat mustache," a reminder of Hitler
n eye, bright blue," a reference to the Nazi's idea that
l, blue-eyed Aryan race was superior to others (44); "Pan
an for armored tank (45); "swastika" (46); "Fascist" (48);
kampf," the title of Adolf Hitler's autobiography and p
manifesto which in translation means "My Struggle"
allusions depict the father as an evil, domineer
eling man, a "brute" (49, 50). They also show the victim
tormentors as part of worldwide problems and situat:
y" is full of in Nazi/Jewish imagery: "German tongue"
wire snare" (28); "Dachau, Auschwitz, Belsen," sites of W
I German death camps (33); "Luftwaffe," the German air f
rld War II (42); "neat mustache," a reminder of Hitler
n eye, bright blue," a reference to the Nazi's idea that
l, blue-eyed Aryan race was superior to others (44); "Pan
an for armored tank (45); "swastika" (46); "Fascist" (48);
kampf," the title of Adolf Hitler's autobiography and p
manifesto which in translation means "My Struggle"
allusions depict the father as an evil, domineer
ling man, a "brute" (49, 50). They also show the victim
ormentors as part of worldwide problems and situat:
incorporates two additional images, the devil and a
to show the evils of domination; in particular, the
d by a patriarchal society that marginalizes women. "Da

Introduction

SYLVIA PLATH is revered as one of the most talented American writers in the twentieth century. This gifted woman suffered from physical and mental illness for much of her life, and yet she faithfully wrote her creative works and cared for her husband, British poet Ted Hughes, and their two children. She was only thirty years old when she took her life on February 11, 1963, in London. During her lifetime, she was a relatively unknown writer, although she had published both a book of poetry, *The Colossus*, in 1960, and a novel, *The Bell Jar*, printed under the pseudonym of Victoria Lucas, in 1963. After her suicide, Plath became an icon, a symbol of a suffering poet who was victimized by a patriarchal society and an adulterous husband. When her second book of poems, *Ariel*, appeared in England in 1965, she achieved literary fame as people eagerly read her poems, regarding them as suicide notes written by a "confessional" poet. By the time *The Bell Jar* appeared in America in 1971, Plath's name was known in nearly every household, and Plath groupies had formed fan clubs. Everything written by Plath sold well. In 1982, nearly twenty years after her death, she won the Pulitzer Prize in Poetry for *The Collected Poems*. Although Plath died almost half a century ago, she remains a beloved writer. Her works are hailed by feminists and admired by people of both sexes for their powerful display of emotions, masterful artistry, and independent voice.

SYLVIA PLATH WAS JUST SEVENTEEN HERSELF WHEN HER FIRST STORY WAS PUBLISHED IN A 1950 ISSUE OF *SEVENTEEN* MAGAZINE. HOWEVER, HER WORK DIDN'T BECOME WILDLY POPULAR UNTIL SHE COMMITTED SUICIDE IN 1963.

Chapter 1

The Life of Sylvia Plath

TO A CASUAL ACQUAINTANCE, the thirty-year-old Sylvia Plath in 1963 would have appeared to "have it all." She was beautiful—tall and slim, with blonde hair, dark eyes, and a gorgeous face. She was brilliant—a summa cum laude graduate of elite Smith College in Massachusetts, a Fulbright scholar, and a graduate of prestigious Cambridge University of England. She was loved and admired by her mother, friends, teachers, and former colleagues. She had fulfilled two dreams of American women: "the romance of falling in love and making a brilliant marriage . . . [and] the romance of finding a job and making a brilliant career" (Whitehead, 120). The first romance occurred when she met and married her soulmate, a tall, dark, ruggedly handsome poet. With him, she owned a country house south of London where she raised her daughter and son. Her career as a writer was blossoming, bringing to fruition the second romance. Already she had published numerous short stories and poems in national magazines, a book of poems, and a novel; she had just completed a book of poems that she felt were the best she had ever written.

Although externally her life seemed great, something was terribly wrong. One frigid February morning, Plath turned on her gas oven, laid her head on a towel on the open oven door, and inhaled the fumes until she stopped breathing.

Almost at once, death propelled Plath into fame; her works became immediate sensations, and her life came under intense scrutiny. While her writings have found critical acclaim and public adoration, her person has not found the same unqualified esteem. She has been vilified and praised, pitied and chastised.

Plath's life is the story of a woman who achieved success beyond most people's wildest dreams and yet fought demons so great that she could not survive. Learning about her life is not only a fascinating topic, but it is also an important means of understanding her highly personal works.

Childhood, 1932-1942: Parental Role Models

Born in Boston on October 27, 1932, Sylvia Plath was the first child and only daughter of Otto Emil and Aurelia Schober Plath, who were both scholarly and ambitious. Otto Plath was a highly successful self-made man. A German immigrant who came to America in 1900 when he was fifteen, he could read, speak, and write perfectly in his new country's language after one year. By 1903, he decided to get a formal education and enrolled in a Wisconsin preparatory school before attending Northwestern College, graduating in 1910 with a major in classical languages. The young man then moved to Seattle to teach high school German and to study at the University of Washington, where he received his master of arts degree in German in 1912. Soon he was also teaching biology, and in the 1920s, he formally studied biology at Harvard, earning a master of science degree in 1925 and a doctorate of science in 1928. During these years he held a number of prestigious graduate and faculty positions at Columbia, M.I.T., Johns Hopkins, and the universities of Washington and California–Berkeley (Alexander, *Rough Magic*, 16). He became a permanent faculty member at Boston University in 1928 (Wagner-Martin, *Sylvia Plath*, 18). He also researched and wrote, publishing his results in scientific journals. By the time his daughter was born, forty-seven-year-old Otto Plath was a nationally recognized expert on bees.

BOTH AURELIA AND OTTO PLATH WERE WELL-EDUCATED AND AMBI-TIOUS. THEY MET IN 1928 WHEN AURELIA ENROLLED IN ONE OF OTTO'S GERMAN CLASSES AT BOSTON UNIVERSITY IN MASSACHUSETTS.

Aurelia Schober was also ambitious, smart, and talented. Although most American women of the 1920s and 1930s did not go to college, Aurelia not only graduated from college but even attended graduate school at Boston University. The oldest daughter of Austrian immigrants, Aurelia had always been an excellent student who particularly loved literature and dreamed of becoming a fiction writer (Alexander, *Rough Magic*, 19). However, when she entered Boston University as a freshman, instead of majoring in English and German, which were her choices, she enrolled in vocational studies, a field her father felt offered more financial security (Alexander, *Rough Magic*, 13). In 1928, Aurelia received her bachelor's degree, graduating as the top-ranked student in Boston University's College of Practical Arts and Letters. After one year of teaching high school German and English when she was twenty-three years old, Aurelia returned to Boston University to earn a master's degree, signing up for a German class taught by Otto Plath, a tall, handsome, slender, forty-five-year-old intellectual (Alexander, *Rough Magic*, 13, 15). At the end of the year, the professor began courting his former pupil and married her on January 4, 1932, the same day he got a divorce from his first wife.

They led a typical 1930s married life. Otto, according to Aurelia, was the boss because his "Germanic theory that the man should be *der Herr des Hauses* (head of the house) persisted" (*Letters*, 13). A workaholic, his life revolved around his job, while Aurelia devoted herself to her husband, catering to his wishes and burying her own dreams of becoming a novelist.

Nearly ten months after their marriage, Sylvia was born. Even though she was a new mother, Aurelia helped her husband get his dissertation on bees published, using her writing skills to turn her husband's unexciting scientific book into a highly readable work. His internationally known book, *Bumblebees and Their Ways*, appeared in 1934. Although it was praised for its lucidity, which was Aurelia's work, and its scholarship, which was Otto's work, only Otto received credit for the book. With his interest in bees, it is no surprise that he kept bees, a hobby Plath also pursued in her adult years. Her interest in bees is also seen in *Ariel*'s series of bee poems ("The Bee Meeting," "The Arrival of the Bee Box," "Stings," "The Swarm," and "Wintering") and in *The Colossus* poem entitled "The Beekeeper's Daughter."

From the time she was little, Sylvia knew that her parents valued learning, writing, working hard, and pursuing dreams. It was natural that their gifted daughter would embrace these same principles.

On April 27, 1935, when Sylvia was two and a half, her brother, Warren Joseph, was born. The following year

SYLVIA AND HER YOUNGER BROTHER, WARREN, GREW UP NEAR THE
MASSACHUSETTS COAST. PLATH'S MEMORIES OF THE SEA INFLUENCED
SEVERAL OF HER POEMS.

her family moved to Winthrop, Massachusetts, a seaside
town just north of Boston, which was only three miles
from Aurelia's parents' home on Point Shirley. Most of
Sylvia's earliest memories take place by the ocean. Here
she swam in the waves and romped on the beach, free to
explore and play to her heart's content, while her adoring
mother and loving grandparents watched over her. She
loved the ocean, not only as a young child but also as an
adult writer, telling her mother in one of her letters home
that "my ocean-childhood . . . is probably the foundation
of my consciousness" (*Letters*, 346). The sounds, sights,
and smells of the ocean were forever etched in Sylvia's
brain. As an adult she wrote about her seaside years in
such poems as "Point Shirley," "Suicide off Egg Rock,"

"The Hermit at Outermost House," and "Ocean 1212-W," the telephone number of her grandparents.

A very bright child, Sylvia began first grade in the fall of 1937 when she was only four years old. Even at this young age, she excelled in school, earning almost all As (Wagner-Martin, *Sylvia Plath*, 26). Sylvia's life seemed almost ideal, as she studied during the school year, spent summers on the beach, and was loved and doted on by her extended family.

However, the family's happiness was marred by Otto Plath's debilitating illness. Since 1935, he had been sick with an ailment he believed to be lung cancer, an incurable disease (Alexander, *Rough Magic*, 28). Wanting to die quickly, he refused to get medical treatment. As he became sicker, his temperament became worse, and he would often have fits of rage. Since his children's laughter and play bothered him, Aurelia arranged for them to spend most of their time upstairs while Otto occupied the down-stairs, allowing them to visit their father for half an hour a day, during which time they performed for him by singing, reciting poetry, and listing scientific names of insects (Alexander, *Rough Magic*, 28). Because of her heavy workload, Aurelia often sent Sylvia to live with her parents at their ocean home. Although separated, mother and daughter remained close, communicating every day by telephone and by letter, beginning a habit that the two would continue for years (Alexander, *Rough Magic*, 29).

Although he continued to teach at Boston University, it became harder and harder for Otto Plath to continue working. Finally, in August 1940, the professor decided to see a doctor after stubbing his toe and watching it become infected, something that should not happen with lung can-cer. The doctor diagnosed his illness as diabetes, a disease which would have been easily managed if it had been treated a year or two earlier. Now, Otto Plath struggled to save his life. But he did not improve; his left leg developed gangrene because of restricted blood flow and was amputated above the knee on October 12. He declined quickly after this, dying on November 5, 1940 (*Letters*, 25). Though Otto Plath was not warm and affectionate, Sylvia loved her father and felt deserted when he died. When her mother told her of her father's death, the eight-year-old responded, "I'll never speak to God again" (*Letters*, 25).

After Otto Plath's death, Sylvia's mother and grandparents worked hard to give her a fulfilling, happy life. Aurelia, now the sole breadwinner, had to work because Otto had left his family practically destitute. When Aurelia returned to teaching, her parents moved into the Plath home, and Aurelia Schober managed the house— cooking, cleaning, and raising the children.

At eight, Sylvia was already interested in writing and publishing. According to biographer Paul Alexander, "To Sylvia, the single most important day of the summer of 1941, August 11, was the date on which the *Boston Herald* published one of her poems in its children's section, 'The Good Sport Page'—the first time the byline 'Sylvia Plath' appeared in print" (Alexander, *Rough Magic*, 36). Entitled simply "Poem," young Sylvia wrote about crickets and butterflies. Even at this early age, she exhibited an uncommon desire to be a published writer. As Alexander accurately notes, "Submitting creative material to periodicals is not a regular activity of most eight-year-olds" (Alexander, *Rough Magic*, 36).

Wellesley, 1942-1950: Formative Years

When Sylvia was nearly ten, practical Aurelia, having been offered a teaching job at Boston University, decided to move inland to a town closer to Boston. The change, she felt, would also benefit the family because they suffered from diseases which were made worse by the humid ocean air: Aurelia had arthritis and both children experienced recurring bouts of sinusitis (Wagner-Martin, *Sylvia*

Plath, 32). In 1942, Aurelia, Sylvia, Warren, and the Schobers moved to 26 Elmwood Road, Wellesley, Massachusetts, a conservative, upper-middle-class suburb of Boston. Because Aurelia decided that her daughter was too young to enter sixth grade, she had to repeat fifth grade, which Sylvia hated.

The eight years Sylvia spent in Wellesley were formative years in which academic excellence and writing became more and more important to her. She also took piano and viola lessons, joined the Girl Scouts, and attended summer camps (Hall, 3). Sylvia was always a superb student, and, according to her mother, it "was in junior high that she developed work habits and skill in her favorite fields of endeavor, art and writing, winning prizes from the 'scholastic awards' competitions each year" (*Letters*, 31). Later, in the summer following Sylvia's high school graduation, she fulfilled a long-sought-after achievement: after submitting numerous works to the magazine *Seventeen*, her first story, "And Summer Will Not Come Again," was published in its August 1950 issue. That same month, the *Christian Science Monitor* published her poem "Bitter Strawberries," a satirical comment on war.

Although Sylvia seemed to be a well-adjusted teenager, she began developing a social mask, showing herself to the world as a smart, cheerful, highly successful girl while inwardly doubting herself and her place in society, a dual nature that appears predominantly in *The Bell Jar*. Her mother explains that "Sylvia was conscious of the prejudice boys built up among themselves about 'brainy' girls. By the time she was a senior in high school, she had learned to hide behind a façade of light-hearted wit when in a mixed group" (*Letters*, 38). Her high school friends saw her cheerful side and described her affectionately in the year book: "Warm smile. . . . Energetic worker. . . . Bumble Boogie piano special. . . . Clever with chalk and paints. . . . Weekends at Williams. . . . Those fully packed sandwiches. . . . Future writer. . . . Those rejection slips from *Seventeen*. . . . Oh, for a license" (Quoted in Ames, 4). But internally, Sylvia was exploring the less desirable aspects of human beings, and her writings, according to her mother, showed "an examination and analysis of the darker recesses of self" (*Letters*, 35).

Although the teenage Sylvia was concerned with looking good to others, she was her own greatest critic. During her high school years, Sylvia became a perfectionist, setting impossibly high standards for herself and feeling that she was a failure if she did not meet her goals. She admits, "I have erected in my mind an image of myself—idealistic and beautiful. Is not that image, free from blemish, the true self—the true perfection? . . . Never, never will I reach the perfection I long for with all my soul—my painting, my poems, my stories—all poor, poor reflections" (*Letters*, 40).

College Years, 1950-1955: Success and Insanity

The next five years brought continued success for Plath, both as a student and as a writer. But these were also years of stress and self-doubt, which led to a depression so severe that she suffered a nervous breakdown and tried to commit suicide.

As a result of her high academic standing in high school, Plath was accepted by the prestigious and expensive Smith College in Northampton, Massachusetts, the largest women's college in the world at that time. Her fees were paid by the scholarships she earned, one from the Wellesley Smith Club and one endowed by Olive Higgins Prouty, a novelist and later a friend and patron. At Smith, she flourished academically, earning her reputation as a star student by performing brilliantly in her classes; becoming an honors student; earning two Smith poetry

WHILE AT SMITH COLLEGE, PLATH ENTERED AND WON THE FICTION-WRITING CONTEST SPONSORED BY *MADEMOISELLE*. ESTHER, THE PROTAGONIST OF HER NOVEL, *THE BELL JAR*, WINS A SIMILAR CONTEST.

prizes; being elected to Phi Beta Kappa and to Alpha, the Smith College honorary society for the arts; publishing stories and poems in national magazines such as *Mademoiselle, Seventeen,* and *Harper's;* and winning *Mademoiselle* magazine's fiction-writing contest with her short story "Sunday at the Mintons." At the same time, she threw herself into school activities, becoming a class officer; serving on councils, boards, and committees; and working as a member of the editorial board of *The Smith Review,* a literary magazine. A college friend of hers later said that Plath, at this period of time, "couldn't wait for life to come to her. . . . She rushed out to greet it, to make things happen" (Quoted in Ames, 5).

Well-organized and driven to succeed, Plath slaved on her creative writings, placing herself on a strict schedule to write poetry while studying words in her father's red-leather-bound thesaurus. She also meticulously recorded her ideas and experiences in her journal. With a great deal of help from her mother, who served as her typist and agent, Plath sent her completed works to publishers. Although her mother's selfless, supportive acts helped advance her career, they also made Plath uneasy because she now felt that she must excel to please both her mother and herself. She told her mother, "I hope I can continue to lay more laurels at your feet" (*Letters,* 94). She advised her brother that "after extracting her life blood and care for 20 years, we should start bringing in big dividends of joy for her" (*Letters,* 113).

Although she wanted to be a stellar student, a famous writer, and a popular classmate, Plath had a hard time merging these aspects of her life. To fit in, the "remarkably attractive young woman, . . . [who] was impressively tall, almost statuesque" (Steiner, 57), affected a nonbrainy demeanor. Nancy Hunter Steiner, Plath's college roommate from 1954 to 1955, notes that her "clothes and manner seemed deliberately cultivated to disguise any distinction. She did not project any rebellious desire to appear different or to accent her intellectual superiority" (Steiner, 56–57). Although to some of her classmates, Plath seemed "cool, aloof, or distant," her roommate is sure that "they were describing only the façade—the barricade that Sylvia erected so that she herself could decide the quality and duration of her relationships. To those who knew her well she was warm, direct, and vulnerable" (Steiner, 59). But, in spite of her attempt to look like a conventional Smith coed, her roommate recognized that "at her core, Sylvia experienced a welter of raging emotions and violent impulses, and on the surface, to keep them in check, she wore the mantle of a bourgeois lady, as inhibiting and restraining as a straight jacket [sic]" (Steiner, 61).

During these years, Plath was often emotionally distraught, physically sick, angry, and hostile. One source of anxiety was the pressure she felt to excel at school. She recognized that in order to keep her scholarships, and therefore continue attending Smith, she had to receive good grades all the time, which she achieved through hard work and long hours of studying. But, in spite of her spectacular achievements, Plath was filled with self-doubt, telling herself, "You are crucified by your own limitations" (*Unabridged Journals*, 154), and admitting, "I do not know who I am, where I am going" (*Unabridged Journals*, 149).

Plath also worried about finding the right guy to marry, something society expected of all women in the 1950s. Like other Smith students, she spent many weekends at men's colleges dating desirable young men. Of particular interest was Dick Norton, a senior science student at Yale who was an old friend from home. During her first year at college, Plath thought he was "the most exciting, smartest, best-looking boy she knew" (Wagner-Martin, *Sylvia Plath*, 68), but by the following summer, she became disillusioned when she learned that he had been intimate with a casual acquaintance. She found it even more distressing that he blamed her for his unfaithfulness, which, he said, "occurred only because *she* had failed him by not coming to Brewster" to visit him (Wagner-Martin, *Sylvia Plath*, 74). Following the double standard of the day, he expected Plath to remain a virgin and forgive him for his affair, an attitude that angered Plath. She fumed in her journal, "For if a man chooses to be promiscuous, he may still aesthetically turn up his nose at promiscuity. He may still demand a woman be faithful to him" (*Unabridged Journals*, 77).

Adding to her anxiety about finding the right husband was her knowledge that when she married, she would be expected to live only through her husband and children, sacrificing her own dreams and ambitions, as her mother had done. In her first college year, Plath confessed, "I dislike being a girl, because as such I must come to realize that I cannot be a man. In other words, I must pour my energies through the direction and force of my mate. My only free act is choosing or refusing that mate" (*Unabridged Journals*, 54). A few months later, she related her fears more vehemently: "I am jealous of men—a dangerous and subtle envy which can corrode, I imagine, any relationship. It is an envy born of the desire to be active and doing, not passive and listening. . . . I am not only jealous; I am vain and proud. I will not submit to having my life fingered by my husband, enclosed in the larger circle of his activity, and nourished vicariously by tales of his actual exploits. I must have a legitimate field of my own, apart from his, which he must respect" (*Unabridged Journals*, 98–99).

Although these external pressures contributed to Plath's anxieties and depressions during her college years, it is also likely that a menstrual disorder, unknown to Plath, caused many of her problems. Plath's bouts of

happiness and depression, which became more pronounced during her college years, happened cyclically
every month, according to Catherine Thompson in her
1990 essay, "'Dawn Poems in Blood': Sylvia Plath and
PMS." Thompson notes that approximately two to three
weeks of elation were followed by two to three weeks of
dejection, symptoms that may result from an acute form
of premenstrual syndrome, or PMS. Plath was affected by
emotional problems, including "irritability, anxiety, tension, mood swings, hostility and depression," as well as
chronic physical conditions, such as "sinusitis, rhinitis,
insomnia, headaches, sore throats, increased need for
sleep, nausea, vomiting, changes in appetite, clumsiness,
backaches, cold sores, conjunctivitis, itchiness, ringing in
the ears, diminished sense of hearing and smell, shakiness,
feelings of suffocation, hot flashes and heart palpitations"
(Thompson, 222–223). These are all symptoms of this disorder that, in its extreme form, can be debilitating. A
number of scholars concur with Thompson. For example,
Diane Middlebrook writes that "Plath's journal has fur-
nished significant evidence for the argument that Plath's
mood swings were symptoms of a chronic menstrual
disorder" (111).

As evidenced in her journals and letters, Plath certainly
had the symptoms of such a disorder, exhibiting almost a
Jekyll-and-Hyde personality. In the summer of 1950, just
before she started college, seventeen-year-old Plath wrote,
"God, is this all it is, the ricocheting down the corridor of
laughter and tears? Of self-worship and self-loathing? Of
glory and disgust?" (*Unabridged Journals*, 17). A little
over a year later, on October 17, 1951, she echoed this
idea: "I don't know why I should be so hideously gloomy,
but I have that miserable 'nobody-loves-me' feeling. . . .
Siniusitis [sic] plunges me in manic depression. But at
least the lower I go the sooner I'll reach bottom & start
the upgrade again [sic]" (*Unabridged Journals*, 533–534).

The following year, she again records her alternating bouts of depression and elation, writing on November 3, 1952, "God, if ever I have come close to wanting to commit suicide, it is now" (*Unabridged Journals*, 149). Eleven days later, she described her change in mood: "I had lost all perspective; I was wandering in a desperate purgatory (with a gray man in a gray boat in a gray river: an apathetic Charon dawdling upon a passionless phlegmatic River Styx . . . and a petulant Christ child bawling on the train) . . . . Tomorrow I will finish my science, start my creative writing story" (*Unabridged Journals*, 153). Almost always, Plath chastised herself for her moodiness and tried to force herself to be optimistic and productive.

In spite of mood swings, Plath was extremely productive and successful in her third year of college. "She sold three poems to *Harper's* for $100; won two Smith poetry prizes for $120; won third prize in *Seventeen*'s fiction contest with 'Initiation'; sold a poem called 'Mad Girls' Love Song' to *Mademoiselle*, and was doing well in that magazine's College Board contest" (Wagner-Martin, *Sylvia Plath*, 95).

Until the end of her junior year, she was able to deal with the anxieties of college life, writing that one should "*never* . . . commit suicide, because something unexpected always happens" (*Letters*, 58). These are words she did not remember for long.

When she finished her third year of college, Plath looked forward to spending the month of June in New York City working as a guest editor for a magazine and then taking a writing course at Harvard. But her vacation did not go as she planned. The events of the summer and fall of 1953 that led to her crash are vividly described in her novel, *The Bell Jar*.

In June, Sylvia joined nineteen other ambitious young college women in New York City to work on the college issue of *Mademoiselle*. At first, she was thrilled, writing in

PLATH ADMIRED DYLAN THOMAS, A WELSH POET LIVING IN NEW YORK IN THE 1950s. SHE HOPED TO MEET HIM WHILE SHE WORKED IN NEW YORK CITY FOR *MADEMOISELLE*.

her scrapbook, "After being one of the two national winners of *Mademoiselle*'s fiction contest ($500!) last August, I felt that I was coming home again when I won a guest editorship representing Smith & took a train to NYC for a salaried month working—hatted & heeled—in *Mlle*'s air conditioned Madison Ave. offices. . . . Fantastic, fabulous, and all other inadequate adjectives go to describe the four gala and chaotic weeks I worked as guest managing Ed . . . living in luxury at the Barbizon [an upscale hotel for women], I edited, met celebrities, was fêted and feasted by a galaxy of UN delegates, simultaneous interpreters & artists . . . an almost unbelievable merry-go-round month" (Quoted in Ames, 5).

Although she wrote about her New York experience very positively, she was not really happy. Almost immediately, she was disappointed when she was assigned to be managing editor instead of fiction editor, as she had hoped. And she exhibited weird behavior, such as "experiencing burns all over her arms in empathy for the Rosenbergs who were . . . being electrocuted," becoming so obsessed with wanting to meet Dylan Thomas that "she hung out in his favorite tavern and lurked in the hall by his hotel-room door," and throwing all of her clothes off the roof of her hotel (Alexander, *Rough Magic*, 113–115). Her month in New York left her both enthusiastic and uncomfortable. She wrote to her brother, "I have been very ecstatic, horribly depressed, shocked, elated, enlightened, and enervated" (*Letters*, 117). When she returned home at the end of June, she was exhausted and miserable, telling her family, "I will let you know what train my coffin will come in on" (*Letters*, 120).

Back home, she was devastated when she found out she had been rejected from a fiction-writing class at Harvard, which made her feel like a complete failure. She sank further into depression. At her mother's suggestion, she decided to spend the rest of the summer reading and learning shorthand so that she would have a marketable skill, but her depression overwhelmed her. First, she could not concentrate; soon she could not sleep; then she could not read; finally, she could not write even simple letters on a piece of paper. Angry with herself, she wrote that she was an "Over-grown, Over-protected, Scared, Spoiled Baby" (*Unabridged Journals*, 543). Worried, Aurelia Plath took her to a psychiatrist, but his electric shock treatments, which were administered poorly, made Plath worse. On August 24, Plath decided to take her own life. Writing a note to her mother stating that she had gone on a long walk, she broke into a locked box, took a bottle of sleeping pills, crept into a crawl space in her basement, swallowed a huge number of pills, and fell unconscious. On August 26, Plath was found alive, surviving only because her body had rejected the pills and vomited many of them up (Alexander, *Rough Magic*, 124). She told her mother that her attempted suicide was "my last act of love" (*Letters*, 126), an act committed because she feared that she could not live up to others' expectations of her.

After spending some time in a state hospital, she was admitted to a private psychiatric hospital, a move made possible because of the generosity of her college scholarship benefactress, Olive Higgins Prouty, who paid all the bills. In the 1950s, cures for mental illness were extremely limited. Even today, it is often difficult to discover and treat the underlying cause of a breakdown. Although recent psychiatrists have diagnosed Plath as either "bipolar"—a brain disorder that consists of extreme mood swings, also known as manic-depressive illness—or as "schizoaffective with predominately depressive features" (quoted in Middlebrook, 111)—a disorder that combines schizophrenia and manic-depressive episodes—they have not determined the reason for her mental illness. Biographer Paul Alexander speculates that Plath inherited a tendency toward this disease. He acquired from Plath's mother the information "that in the Plath family their mother, a sister, and a niece all suffered from depression" and that "Otto's mother had become so sick that she had been hospitalized" (*Rough Magic*, 135).

No matter what the cause of her breakdown, Sylvia was lucky that, from the start, her new doctor at the private hospital understood her problems and successfully treated the symptoms of the disease. Prouty wrote to Aurelia Plath, "Dr. B. suggested that she is a perfectionist, which accounts for her self-depreciation if she falls short of perfection in anything she does" (*Letters*, 128). The doctor tried to teach Plath to trust herself, to understand that she did not need to achieve to be loved, and to realize that "her desperate and nearly insatiable demands for recognition through success were bound to meet with failure" (Wagner-Martin, *Sylvia Plath*, 109). With psychotherapy given by this compassionate doctor, insulin shock treatments, and correctly administered electric shock treatments, Plath began to improve. She later described this period of her life as "a time of darkness, despair, disillusion—so black only as the inferno of the human mind can be—symbolic death, and numb shock—then the painful agony of slow rebirth and psychic regeneration" (quoted in Ames, 8). By the end of the year, Plath was well enough to return to Smith for the second semester.

But she was not quite the same young woman who had left school several months earlier. Now she no longer merely "chafed under a superimposed behavioral code that was both stringent and ambiguous" (Steiner, 110), but she went about defying the accepted norms for females. Her friend Steiner explains that although she "wanted desperately to live up to the expectations of a society that viewed her as a bright, charming, enormously talented disciple of bourgeois conformity . . . she ached to

PLATH WAS AWARDED A PRESTIGIOUS FULBRIGHT FELLOWSHIP, WHICH ENABLED HER TO ATTEND GRADUATE SCHOOL AT CAMBRIDGE UNIVERSITY IN ENGLAND.

experience life in all its grim and beautiful complexity" (97). Determined to have the same freedom as men, she became sexually active, sometimes becoming involved in dangerous relationships. Steiner regarded Plath's displays of promiscuity and the "eccentricities of her behavior as personality problems or remnants of immaturity or human imperfections, not as symptoms of emotional illness" (99).

Although Steiner had been good friends with Plath for

almost a year, it was not long before she set limits on their friendship, finding Plath too demanding of her time and too self-centered. This happened in the summer of 1954 when the two young women were attending Harvard. On the morning Steiner had final exams, Plath woke up with a headache, shrieking, "My head is flying off. . . . I can't stand the pain. Do something; I'm dying" (Steiner, 99). Although Steiner dutifully found a doctor who was willing to make a house call, Plath seemed totally dependent on her friend, fervently insisting that she remain with her until the doctor came. But Steiner, not wishing to fail her class, left to take her exam when another roommate was able to care for Plath. From then on, Steiner drew back from Plath, realizing that she could not be fully responsible for her friend's well-being.

Plath finished college the next academic year. Her senior year brought her more recognition, more awards and prizes, and more publications. In June 1955, she graduated summa cum laude from Smith College and, having been awarded a Fulbright fellowship, prepared to travel to England to study at Newnham College at Cambridge University.

Marriage and Career, 1955-1962: Fulfillment

During the next seven years, Plath lived a life that promised her great happiness personally and professionally. She undertook graduate studies at Cambridge in English literature, receiving a second bachelor's degree, the equivalent of a master's in America; traveled extensively; wrote profusely; and married the man of her dreams.

At Cambridge, Plath was, as usual, an excellent student. She also took time to do creative writing and participate in extracurricular activities—acting in the Dramatic Society, joining a political group, and writing for the school newspaper, *Varsity*. She dated regularly, and

PLATH MET TED HUGHES DURING HER FIRST YEAR AT CAMBRIDGE UNIVERSITY. THE TWO POETS DATED FOR ONLY FOUR MONTHS BEFORE MARRYING IN JUNE 1956; PLATH WAS TWENTY-THREE AND HUGHES WAS TWENTY-FIVE.

traveled in Europe during Christmas break.

On February 25, 1956, she met a man who changed her life forever—British poet Ted Hughes. From the beginning, Hughes and Plath were intensely attracted to each other. On the night they met, Plath writes, "he kissed me bang smash on the mouth and ripped my hairband off, my lovely red hairband scarf which has weathered the sun and much love, and whose like I shall never again find, and my favorite silver earrings: hah, I shall keep, he barked" (*Unabridged Journals*, 212).

Hughes, the youngest of three children, was two years older than Plath, born on August 17, 1930, in West Yorkshire, England, where his father worked as a tobacconist. In the secluded English countryside, Ted enjoyed hunting and fishing and, like his mother, was interested in the occult and witchcraft. He did his National Service working as a ground wireless mechanic in the Royal Air Force for two years. He graduated from Cambridge in 1954 with an anthropology degree and took odd jobs laboring as a chauffeur, gardener, and night watchman (Alexander, *Rough Magic*, 196). According to Linda Wagner-Martin, he and Plath were well suited to each other. They shared a love for the same writers—such as Chaucer, Shakespeare, Donne, Blake, Yeats, Hopkins, Lawrence, and Dylan Thomas, and they possessed "a deep understanding of the power of language (especially Ted, with his boyhood in the Yorkshire dialect), as well as that of mythology and folklore" (*Sylvia Plath*, 132). That spring they spent every day together, and on June 16, 1956, Hughes and Plath married. For the rest of the summer they honeymooned in Spain, renting rooms in a small village on the Mediterranean Sea. From the beginning, the two poets carved out time to be apart every day so that each could spend time writing alone. Plath adored and admired her husband, finding him "a magnificent handsome brilliant husband" whose "mind is the biggest, most imaginative" she had ever met (*Unabridged Journals*, 249).

When they returned to Cambridge, Ted taught at a boys' school, while Plath, with her Fulbright scholarship renewed, finished her studies and continued writing and publishing her works. In January 1957, she had a number of items appear: a story in the Cambridge magazine *Granta*, six poems in *Poetry*, and one in *Atlantic Monthly*.

Although her own writing remained extremely important to her, Plath now, like her mother, took on the duties of helping her husband succeed—typing Ted's poems, submitting them for publication, and serving as his literary agent. When his first book of poetry was accepted for publication in February 1957, she gushed, "I am more happy than if it was my book published! I have worked so closely on these poems of Ted's and typed them so many countless times through revision after revision that I feel ecstatic about it all. I am so happy *his* book is accepted *first*. . . . I can rejoice, then, much more, knowing Ted is ahead of me" (*Letters*, 297). She also believed that their marriage helped both of them, proclaiming that "he is the perfect male counterpart of my own self," and declaring that "we are the most faithful, creative, healthy simple couple imaginable!" (*Unabridged Journals*, 271).

After completing her Cambridge studies, she and Ted, who was fed up with teaching, a job he found too demanding because it robbed him of writing time, moved to the United States in 1957, where Plath had accepted a job at Smith College teaching freshman English.

Now it was Plath's turn to feel the aggravation her husband had felt. Alexander writes that "From the start, Plath found teaching painful. She felt inadequate for the task, overwhelmed by the material, and intimidated by the girls" (*Rough Magic*, 209). Teaching drained her energies, and she "lost all drive to write" as "an emotional—not a physical—exhaustion set in" (*Rough Magic*, 210). After half a year of teaching, she described her life as "a grim grind" (*Unabridged Journals*, 323). As she began to get more depressed, she depended more and more on her husband, relating that on one day "she sought out Ted in the apartment some one hundred times, on each occasion to kiss or, merely, smell him. Soon she concluded that her desire to be near Ted had become as fundamental to her as eating" (Alexander, *Rough Magic*, 215). Although Plath was unhappy with her job, her colleagues were delighted with her teaching, finding her "one of the two or three finest instructors ever to appear in the English department at Smith College" (Quoted in Ames, 8).

Adding to her frustrations was Ted's success. With no job to tie him down, Ted had plenty of time to write, and he was receiving much critical praise for his work. This, according to Alexander, caused Plath, who was "in a hell of lecturing and paper grading," to become "jealous of him for the first time" (*Rough Magic*, 210). As she grew more and more frustrated, friction developed between the two, and they picked on each other about minor things. After one year, Plath left teaching, giving up her childhood plan of being an English professor. She and Hughes decided to live with financial uncertainty so that both could fulfill their dreams of being full-time writers, and they moved to a small apartment in Boston in 1958.

Because of her financial worries, Plath took two part-time jobs that year, in the fall working as a secretary at Massachusetts General Hospital's psychiatric clinic (the same hospital in which she had been a patient in 1953), and in the spring, working as a secretary for the chairman of the department of Sanskrit and Indian Studies at Harvard University (Alexander, *Rough Magic*, 223, 230). These jobs provided material for two of her works, "The Daughters of Blossom Street" and "Johnny Panic and the Bible of Dreams."

As the year passed, Plath had reason to question her decision to try to be a full-time writer because even though she had time to write, she could not. Over and over again in her journal, she despaired about her writer's block and urged herself to write. On September 14, she ordered herself, "Must work & get out of paralysis" (*Unabridged Journals*, 421). Nearly two weeks later, she lamented "the sense of nothing written, nothing read, nothing done" (*Unabridged Journals*, 423). Her inability to write led to depression, and, according to Alexander, she "sought targets on whom she could vent the anger. She complained to Ted about money, his poor hygiene— she could not abide his dirty hair, his ragged fingernails, his disinclination for bathing—and her inability to become pregnant, something she now desperately wanted" (Alexander, *Rough Magic*, 223). Aurelia was also her victim, as Plath now considered her mother a cause of her depression. She reasoned that her mother's constant worries about her caused her to become angry, an emotion that led to her depression. This view was encouraged by Sylvia's psychiatrist, who told her patient, "I give you permission to hate your mother." Plath then often began to say, "I hate my mother" (Alexander, *Rough Magic*, 224). In her journals, Plath, however, was more rational, writing, "I may hate her, but that's not all, I pity and love her too" (445).

The Hugheses' once happy romantic life began to fade during this time as they fought more frequently. One cause of disagreement was over the expected roles of the male and female. Although Plath did all of the cooking and cleaning, Ted wanted her to do more, and he resorted to humiliating her in front of friends to get his way, complaining that Plath would "hide shirts, rip up torn socks, never sew on buttons." Later he told her that he shamed her so he could force her to do these jobs: "I thought that would make you do it!" Plath speculates that the reason for the fight was that, "Both of us must feel partly that the other isn't filling a conventional role: he isn't 'earning bread and butter' in any reliable way, I'm not 'sewing on buttons and darning socks' by the hearthside. He hasn't even got us a hearth; I haven't even sewed a button" (*Unabridged Journals*, 444–445). Since they were living on a shoestring budget, it is understandable that they also fought about money. On December 26, 1958, Plath reveals, "I do fight with Ted: two acrid fights. The real reasons: we both worry about money: we have enough till

PLATH BECAME FRIENDS WITH ANNE SEXTON—A CONTEMPORARY POET WHOSE GREATEST FAME WOULD ALSO COME AFTER SHE COMMITTED SUICIDE—WHILE ATTENDING A POETRY CLASS AT BOSTON UNIVERSITY IN MASSACHUSETTS.

next September 1st. Then what? How to keep concerns about money and profession from destroying the year we have?" (*Unabridged Journals*, 445).

By early 1959, Plath's life became happier when she attended Robert Lowell's poetry class at Boston University and became friends with two other poets, Anne Sexton and George Starbuck.

But her writer's block continued. On March 20, 1959,

she grieved, "Writing impossible as my one thing, it is so dried up" (*Unabridged Journals*, 474). Later that month, March 29, 1959, she anguished, "I have a vision of the poems I would write, but do not. When will they come?" (*Unabridged Journals*, 476). The following month things were no better: "I am still blocked about prose. A novel still scares me" (*Unabridged Journals*, 477). Those pieces she had written, she could not get published, declaring on June 6, 1959, "I am grim, sour. Rejection will follow rejection. I am only a little better equipped to take them than a year, two years ago" (*Unabridged Journals*, 492).

By now, the Hugheses had been in America for two years, and Ted was anxious to return to his home country. He had been awarded a Guggenheim grant, a substantial amount of money, so that he could spend a year writing. Furthermore, Plath was finally pregnant, and Ted wanted his child to be born in England. Plath, too, was excited to move to England. Before leaving, the two poets traveled to California to meet Plath's Aunt Frieda, Otto's sister. During the fall of 1959, they lived in Yaddo, New York, at an artist's colony. Here Plath, with Ted's guidance, wrote many of the poems that were later published in her book, *The Colossus*. Writing copiously and feeling no monetary worries, Plath and Hughes got along well. She praised her husband as her "salvation," finding him "so rare, so special" (*Unabridged Journals*, 517). After spending Thanksgiving with Aurelia Plath, the Hugheses sailed for England.

At their tiny apartment close to Regent's Park, both writers spent a great deal of time writing and reading. They also led an active social life, developing many new friendships. In 1960, Plath's first big excitement was signing a contract with a British publisher for a book of poetry, *The Colossus and Other Poems*. She was also happy that Ted's second volume of poetry was published.

But of greatest importance was the birth of their daughter, Frieda Rebecca Hughes, on April 1, 1960.

Now, as a wife, mother, and secretary for her husband, Plath found little time to write. More and more, she became frustrated with her unfulfilling creative life and her stifling role as a submissive marriage partner. Instead of being known as Sylvia Plath, excellent scholar and talented writer, most of their new acquaintances knew her only as Ted's wife. One of their new friends, A. Alvarez, later noted, "Sylvia seemed effaced, the poet taking a back seat to the young mother and housewife" (6). Being regarded as only an extension of her husband, a typical attitude in the 1950s and 1960s, she was lonesome, writing, "I have so missed a good American girl friend!" (*Letters*, 383).

Meanwhile, Ted was thriving. He was able to write daily because he had a quiet retreat at the home of friends. A fairly well-known poet, he was in demand for readings, his works were published copiously, and he won a variety of awards. Understandably, Plath became somewhat jealous, wistfully remarking, "I really hunger for a study of my own out of hearing of the nursery where I could be alone with my thoughts for a few hours a day" (*Letters*, 392). Her disappointment with her life became keener after the publication of *The Colossus and Other Poems* in November because it was hardly noticed by critics and it received no awards. Adding to her anguish was her poor health. In February 1961, she miscarried; that same month she had an appendectomy.

After a dismal winter, the spring brought her renewed joy. Professionally, things were looking up for her: she found a study for herself in London and began writing *The Bell Jar*; the prestigious *New Yorker* offered her a long-term contract for her poems; and the U.S. publisher Alfred A. Knopf agreed that they would publish *The Colossus*. Personally, her life also improved. After the devastating

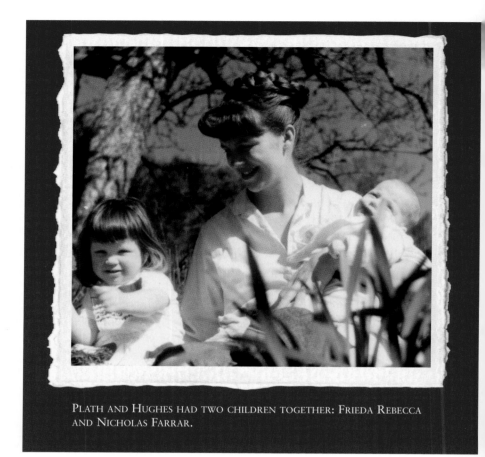

PLATH AND HUGHES HAD TWO CHILDREN TOGETHER: FRIEDA REBECCA AND NICHOLAS FARRAR.

miscarriage, she was pregnant again, and she and Ted decided to buy a large home in the country where they would both have space to write. In September 1961, they purchased an old, run-down, thatch-roofed manor house in Devon, located south of London about an hour's drive from the ocean.

At first, life in the country seemed almost ideal, as home and professional life blended well together. Professionally, Plath was able to flourish because she and Ted took turns caring for Frieda, allowing Plath to write in the mornings and Hughes in the afternoons. Besides composing creative works, she also edited an anthology of American poets for the *Critical Quarterly*. In November, she was awarded a Saxton fellowship of $2,080 from Harper and Brothers, giving her money to hire a babysitter so she could spend more time on her novel. She was also fulfilled on a personal level: on January 17, 1962, Nicholas Farrar Hughes was born.

The Breakup, 1962: Devastation

During the spring of 1962, Plath continued dividing her days between domestic and professional activities. In the afternoons, she took horseback riding lessons, picked and sold hundreds of daffodils, and entertained guests. In the mornings, she wrote. She completed a radio play for the BBC entitled *Three Women*, which featured three women who discuss pregnancy, miscarriage, and birth.

In spite of the seemingly idyllic life, Plath seemed to sense that something was wrong with her marriage. The bitter times began in May. *The Colossus and Other Poems* was finally published in the United States. When only one review appeared in the first four months, Plath was distressed. After slaving over this book for years, she realized that she would receive no money and no fame for her efforts, which caused her to question her worth as a writer.

Also in May, she began to question her value as a female when Ted had an affair with another woman even though Plath had been faithful to him. The young couple who had rented the Hugheses' apartment in London, David and Assia Gutmann Wevill, came for a weekend visit in the middle of May. Almost immediately, "an odd chemistry formed between Ted and Assia; their interaction began to take on obvious sexual overtones" (Alexander, *Rough Magic*, 278). Although Plath witnessed their stolen glances and heard their suggestive words, she did not know that when the Wevills left their home, Ted had given

Assia a note: "I must see you tomorrow in London" (Alexander, *Rough Magic*, 277).

Plath, meanwhile, went on with her life as normal, even enjoying a new hobby: raising bees. In early June, she gushed to her mother, "This is the richest and happiest time of my life" (*Letters*, 455), as she spent time with her babies, ambled through the beautiful countryside, and glowed with pride over Ted's successes. However, when Plath's mother visited in June, she saw firsthand that her daughter's marriage was faltering. Despite her denials, Plath also seemed to sense this, writing a poem about a failing relationship, "The Other," in early July. But she continued to act as if her life were ideal, even though she often did not know where Ted was (he now frequently went to London alone), and even though they argued more than they ever had. On the morning of July 9, while Ted took care of the babies so she and her mother could shop in Exeter, Plath reiterated her belief that her life was perfect, telling her mother, "I have everything in life I've ever wanted—a wonderful husband, two adorable children, a lovely home, and my writing" (*Letters*, 458).

By that afternoon, her world was shattered. Plath and her mother returned home earlier than expected. Hearing the telephone ring, Plath rushed to answer it before the caller hung up; Ted, at the top of the stairs, also raced to pick it up, running down the steps so quickly that he missed a step and fell backward down half a flight of stairs. When Plath calmly answered the phone, the caller, clearly a woman, lowered her voice to try to sound like a man, and asked for Ted. Plath was not fooled; she knew the voice was Assia Gutmann Wevill's. She gave the phone to Ted, who talked briefly and hung up. Fully aware of what the call meant, Plath furiously ripped the telephone wire out of the wall. That evening, she drove to see her best friend, Elizabeth Compton, who was shocked by

Plath's mental condition and remembered the visit years later: "She told me that Ted was in love with another woman, that she knew Assia and was terrified of her. She wept and wept and held onto my hands, saying, 'Help me!' . . . But the most frightening thing she said was, 'When you give someone your whole heart and he doesn't want it, you cannot take it back. It's gone forever'" (Quoted in Alexander, *Rough Magic*, 284).

As the days passed, Plath's anger increased. In a fit of rage, she built a bonfire in her yard and, with her mother watching, ripped up her new novel, a sequel to *The Bell Jar* that told the story of the heroine's return to health after a happy marriage, and threw it into the fire. She continued to purge her life by casting papers into bonfires, one day burning about a thousand letters from her mother. Another day she destroyed many of Ted's belongings, including letters, drafts of poems, and boxes of waste paper, dancing while the papers were reduced to ashes (Alexander, *Rough Magic*, 286).

August 4, 1962, the day Aurelia left Devon, was the last time she would see her daughter.

With her mother gone and Ted spending more time in London with Assia, Plath became more and more depressed. One day she drove her car off the road, maybe an accident or possibly a purposeful act to try to harm herself. By August 27, she told her mother that, even though she did not believe in divorce, she was going to get a legal separation because she was unwilling to live this "degraded and agonized life" (*Letters*, 460). But in September, she decided to try for reconciliation. Hughes and Plath traveled to Ireland; however, Ted suddenly left Plath and returned to London, where Assia lived.

Besides her anguish over Ted's desertion, Plath also dreaded disappointing her mother. According to her friend Jillian Becker, she was infuriated by what she was sure her mother's reaction would be: that she was a failure. All of her life she had spent trying to impress her mother "with success after success" (Becker, 29). Therefore, she refused to return to Wellesley when her mother invited her and the babies to come and live with her, informing Aurelia, "I cannot face you again until I have a new life" (*Letters*, 465).

To try to cope with losing Ted, Plath began a writing frenzy that lasted throughout the fall. She rose early every day, forcing herself to write from 4 a.m. to 8 a.m. every morning, no matter how exhausted she was. The first week of October, she wrote five poems on bees. On October 12, the day after Ted left for good, she composed her angry poem "Daddy," which concludes with the words, "I'm through." Other poems followed quickly: "Medusa," a poem about a woman who is wronged by a monster; "The Jailer," a work about a woman so angry with a man that she wants him "dead or away"; and "Lesbos," a monologue about home life gone wrong. By now, Plath was sick with a high fever, inspiring "Fever 103°." Poem after poem hurriedly spewed forth: "Amnesiac," "Lyonnesse," "Cut," "By Candlelight," "Poppies in October," "Ariel," and "Lady Lazarus." Unlike earlier times of writing, her words came so quickly that she was composing, as she declared, "a poem a day before breakfast. . . . Terrific stuff as if domesticity had choked me" (*Letters*, 466). In October, she enthusiastically announced, "I am writing the best poems of my life" (*Letters*, 468).

Another huge breakthrough occurred during the fall of 1962: *The Bell Jar* was accepted for publication in England. By December, she had finished thirty poems, which she planned to group together as a book of poetry, and had begun writing another novel. In spite of her productivity, she was miserable and angry, raging against her unfaithful husband. Her isolation in Devon also depressed her; feeling totally alone, she cried that she was "stuck down here, as into a sack I fight for air and freedom and the culture and libraries of a city" (*Letters*, 465). Because of her misery and her hectic writing schedule, it is no wonder that Plath kept getting sick with a high fever and flu, which added to her sense of hopelessness. In October, she struggled to survive, writing, "Am fighting now against hard odds and alone" (*Letters*, 469). Realizing she needed to return to health, she planned to take a vacation in Ireland so she could recover near the ocean, and then she intended to move to London with her babie,s where she would receive stimulation from a cultural environment and support from friends. Her plans to go to Ireland never materialized, but she did move to London in December 1962. Her apartment seemed perfect for her because it was the former home of poet W. B. Yeats.

At first, it seemed as if she might get better. Staying busy, she worked on her *Ariel* poems and the new novel, made several BBC broadcasts, and received acceptance notices for a number of poems. Shortly after moving to London, in December 1962, she wrote, "The next five years of my life look heavenly—school terms in London, summer in Devon" (*Letters*, 490).

Final Days, 1963: Under the Bell Jar

Plath struggled with depression and the flu throughout January. When *The Bell Jar*, printed under the pseudonym Victoria Lucas, appeared in January 1963, Plath was distressed because the reviews were not as enthusiastic as she had hoped. Her plight was made worse by the frigid winter weather, the coldest one in London since the winter of 1813–1814. Pipes froze, so there often was no water, and light and heat went off with no warning (Butscher, 352–353). According to Frances McCullough, editor of Plath's journals, by January 1963 "Plath was in extremis; her marriage to poet Ted Hughes was over, she was in a panic about money, and had moved to a bare flat in

London with her two small children in the coldest British winter in a hundred years. All three of them had the flu, there was no phone, and there was no help with child care" (x–xi). Still she persevered with her writings, slaving on her *Ariel* poems every morning before eight when her children woke up even though, according to critic Lois Ames, "the sense of human experience as horrid and ungovernable, the sense of all relationships as puppetlike and meaningless, had come to dominate her imagination" (14).

Plath tried to recover from her deep depression. Following the advice of her doctor, she took prescribed sedatives. She sought help from her former psychiatrist in Boston. She busied herself by visiting friends. But Plath could not recover. The same types of problems faced her that had been present in her earlier breakdown in 1953: "the abrupt departure of the central male figure in her life, critical rejection, . . . isolation in new surroundings, complete exhaustion" (McCullough, xi).

On the days before she killed herself, Plath and her children stayed with her friend Becker, where Plath spent her time resting while Becker cooked and cared for her children. On Saturday night, Plath exerted herself to go out to meet with Ted, and then suddenly, the next day, she decided to go home.

Monday morning, February 11, Plath committed suicide, gassing herself in the oven in her kitchen. She had been careful to take care of her children, ages one and not quite three, before she turned on the gas, placing plates of bread and butter and cups of milk by their beds, and sealing their bedroom door with tape and towels to make sure they could not breathe the fumes. When the nurse, Myra Norris, arrived at 9 a.m., she found Plath's building locked. Unable to get to Plath's upstairs apartment, Norris went to the back of the house to search for another entrance. She saw two children crying in an upstairs window. Now very worried, Norris found Charles Langridge working in the area and enlisted his help to get into the house. Smelling gas coming from Plath's apartment, Langridge broke open Plath's door. They turned off the gas, opened the windows, and carried Plath's body to the living room, where Norris began giving her artificial respiration. Meanwhile, Langridge called the police and, when the officer arrived, helped rescue Plath's children. He also called her doctor, John Horder. At 10:30 a.m., Horder pronounced Plath dead (Alexander, *Rough Magic*, 330–331). The police officer at the coroner's office described her suicide vividly: "She had really meant to die. . . . She'd blocked the cracks at the bottom of the doors to the landing and the sitting room, turned all the gas taps full on, neatly folded a kitchen cloth and placed it on the floor of the oven, and laid her cheek on it" (quoted in Becker, 39). He also reflected that it was a good thing no one had found her and pulled her out because, after some minutes of breathing in gas, her mind would have been "gone forever" and she would have lived as "a vegetable" (quoted in Becker, 40).

The funeral was held in Ted's Yorkshire church. Besides Ted's family, only four people connected to Plath attended: her brother Warren and his wife, and Gerry and Jillian Becker. Aurelia Plath, devastated by her daughter's death, was too ill to travel.

After Plath's death, Ted continued his affair with Assia. Although they lived together, the two never married; in fact, Assia never divorced her husband. Assia and Ted had one daughter, Shura, born in 1967. In March 1969, Assia, holding her toddler, turned on the gas in the oven, killing them both.

Because Plath's death relates to the type of person she was, the reasons for her suicide have been much discussed by her friends, readers, critics, and biographers. Why did she kill herself? Some think she was merely looking for

AFTER PLATH'S DEATH, HER BODY WAS BURIED IN A CEMETERY IN HEPTONSTALL, WEST YORK, ENGLAND. SUPPORTERS AND FANS OF PLATH HAVE REPEATEDLY TRIED TO REMOVE HER MARRIED NAME, HUGHES, FROM THE GRAVESTONE.

sympathy and expected someone to save her at the last minute, but she miscalculated the danger. Those holding this view include Alvarez, a critic and friend of the Hugheses in London (33–38), and Plath's college roommate, Steiner, who years earlier had found Plath too dependent on others. Steiner writes: "I do not believe that Sylvia meant to die, and I suspect that when she did die, on that bleak and lonely February day when she stuck her head into the oven, it was because no one was there to pull her out—to submit to the final macabre threat: 'I'll die if you desert me'" (112). Those holding this view point out that Plath was expecting two visitors that morning, a nurse and a babysitter, either of whom might have rescued her (Middlebrook, 209).

Other analysts suspect that, at least in part, Plath's death may have been a carefully calculated measure to gain lasting fame. Becker relates this chilling thought: "She did, I believe, think of posterity. She probably saw that she could accomplish recognition as a contributor to English literature better by dying than living. . . . Fame was her last desire, as it had been her first. . . . Too much the writer and too little the mother, did she gas herself because the story she invented for her life demanded that ending?" (Becker, 53, 69).

Though most friends and critics feel that Plath killed herself because she was severely depressed, they do not agree on the reasons for her despair. There are, in general, three schools of thought: Plath committed suicide because of her husband's mistreatment, her uncontrollable emotions, or a biological problem.

Many feel that Plath's depression was primarily caused by her husband's adultery. In fact, the first generally accepted view was that Plath was "the pathetic victim of [Ted Hughes's] heartless mistreatment" (Stevenson, xii). Although Plath's doctor did not regard the breakup of her marriage as the sole cause of her depression, he said it was a "very important" factor (Alexander, *Rough Magic*, 325). Becker agrees and implies that Ted himself seemed to be afraid that he was at least partly responsible for her death. Becker says that during the meal that followed Sylvia's funeral service, Ted exchanged words with her, trying to take blame away from himself. Becker recalls, "Hughes blurted out vehemently but quietly . . . 'Everybody hated her.' 'I didn't,' I said. 'It was either her or me,' he said, and was to repeat a number of times that afternoon" (Becker, 44). Becker is sure that Plath's unhappiness over Ted's betrayal was a major cause of her suicide, explaining, "She left no last-minute scribbled note to Hughes, but she left him her poetry, knowing that he would understand those last poems as suicide notes, not apologetic but accusatory. Her death itself was addressed to him, and through him to the world" (Becker, 53).

This position is backed up by later biographers. Wagner-Martin, writing in 1987, makes clear that Plath's suicide occurred because of an "acute depression" caused by "changes in her personal life [Ted's adultery and their impending divorce] that revived earlier fears and depressions" (*Sylvia Plath*, 243). Alexander, in his 1999 biography, concurs and goes further, writing that Hughes, in a letter written to Plath's mother in March 1963, "confesses that his 'madness' played a large part in Plath's final depression, which ended in her suicide. . . . From the letter's tone and subject matter it is clear Hughes felt more than slightly responsible for Plath's death. His guilt is palpable in the letter. If there is an eternity, Hughes ends his letter to Aurelia Plath, he would be 'damned in it'" (*Rough Magic*, xvi).

Besides Hughes's infidelity, many are quick to point out additional external factors contributing to Plath's extreme depression and inability to think clearly: the intensely cold weather, the heavy snows that caused frequent power outages and forced her to remain housebound with her sick babies, and her physical illnesses of flu and sinusitis.

Although many see that circumstances outside of herself, particularly Hughes's adultery, caused Plath's depression, others argue that she was dejected because of her own volatile, vindictive temperament. Plath's first biographer, Edward Butscher, blames Plath alone for her troubles, describing her as a split personality "aching to go on a rampage of destruction against all those who possessed what she did not and who made her cater to their whims" (67). Thus, he asserts that her suicide was a vindictive act against her poor, abused husband. Biographer Anne Stevenson agrees with Butscher that Plath was to blame for her unhappiness; Stevenson writes that Plath was filled with "tense, vulnerable nerves" (109), "paranoia" (131), "self-absorption" (257), and a "childlike, American" philosophy (120). Thus, Stevenson concludes, Hughes was driven to be unfaithful because Plath was too moody: "the inflexibility of [Plath's] self-absorption, coupled with the dark moods that were inseparable from her strange genius, may finally have broken down her husband's defenses" and caused him to commit adultery (257). Biographer Ronald Hayman also suggests that one cause of Plath's suicide was her anger: "In so far as her suicide was an act of aggression, it was aimed against [Hughes] and his new lover, Assia Wevill" (93).

A third school of critics thinks that Plath's depression was caused by some type of biological problem causing her to intentionally, but irrationally, commit suicide. This is the view of Horder, her physician, who believed "she was in the grips of a compulsion attributable to brain chemistry, the biological condition that her psychoactive medication was addressing with gradual efficacy" (Middlebrook, 209–210). What caused the biological problem is not clear, but three primary reasons have been advanced. One suggestion is that Plath once again had a breakdown because of a mental illness she inherited from her father's family (Alexander, *Rough Magic*, 135). Another view is that Plath's disturbed emotional state was caused by a hormone imbalance due to severe PMS, an imbalance made worse from child-bearing and nursing (Thompson, 221–249). If this is the case, Plath's death is extremely tragic, for, in her last letter to her mother, Plath says that her doctor had referred her to "a woman doctor" (*Letters*, 500). According to Thompson, "Katharina Dalton, a London physician, was successfully treating severe cases of PMS with progesterone therapy. . . . [Therefore,] she died in the only city in the world where she could have received effective medical treatment" (244).

Plath's husband and mother both believed that her biological problem was an alteration of her brain chemistry brought about by the prescription drug she was taking for depression, an alteration that caused her to commit suicide. The idea that drugs caused Plath to deteriorate physically was suggested in 1991 by biographer Hayman, who thought she was overdosing on drugs. He writes: "She was obviously exceeding the [recommended] dosage, [which] may well have been the cause of the slurred vowels, the faraway look and the seraphic expression" seen by spectators (194). Plath's mother, however, did not believe that her daughter's problem was caused by an overdose of drugs, but rather by an inconsistent amount of medicine in her system. Knowing that if the drug wore off while her daughter slept, the dosage level would go too low and cause severe problems, she concluded that Plath "should not have been alone," and stated her conviction that her daughter's death "was not a premeditated and desired end, it was really a chemical thing" (quoted in Middlebrook, 210). Hughes also believed Plath died because of drugs, but he thought her brain chemistry was altered by an adverse, allergic reaction to her prescribed tranquilizer. Middlebrook reveals that Hughes, in a private letter written years after his wife's death, stated that "Plath's doctors in America had established that she was 'allergic' to that particular antidepressant; Hughes believed that it induced the suicidal thoughts it was supposed to alleviate—that the medication prompted the suicide, in effect. The whole catastrophe had been brought on by the publication of that 'accursed book' *The Bell Jar*, he said, 'that required the tranquillizers' her doctor prescribed, and that led directly to her death" (Middlebrook, 210).

Although many reasons have been advanced, the exact cause of Plath's suicide remains unknowable. Perhaps the best explanation comes from Plath herself, "To the person in the bell jar, blank and stopped as a dead baby, the world itself is the bad dream" (*The Bell Jar*, 237).

THE UNITED STATES ENTERED WORLD WAR II IN 1941 WHEN PLATH WAS NINE YEARS OLD. MANY OF HER POEMS ALLUDE TO THE WAR, HITLER, AND THE NAZIS.

Chapter 2

Sylvia Plath's Times

SYLVIA PLATH was born in 1932, the year that Americans, devastated by the Great Depression that had begun with the stock market crash of 1929, elected Franklin Delano Roosevelt president of the United States, hoping that his promised New Deal—to provide food and housing for the unemployed and to restore the nation's economy— would alleviate the nation's problems. During the 1930s, many Americans lost their jobs or their life savings when America's economy went through a severe recession as businesses cut production, factories and stores closed, banks failed, and farms were deserted after being reduced to dust during the dry summer of 1934, a plight vividly described by John Steinbeck in *The Grapes of Wrath*. In spite of the widespread misery, Otto Plath continued to be employed as a university professor. As a result, Plath spent her early years in a comfortable, secure environment.

Besides not knowing about the wretchedness of the Great Depression, Sylvia was also unaware that a ruthless, powerful dictator, Adolf Hitler, was in control of Germany. Nor did she know that he and military leaders in Japan began to take control of neighboring countries, beginning in the mid–1930s when she was a preschooler. Their actions finally led to World War II, which began when the Nazis overran Poland on September 1, 1939, and France, Great Britain, and other countries (the Allies) declared war on Germany, and later on Italy and Japan, Germany's Axis partners. However, by the time America entered the war after the Japanese attacked Pearl Harbor on December 7, 1941, nine-year-old Sylvia was well aware of the war. Like others of her generation, Plath spent her "formative years listening to radio newscasts from the battlefronts of the Second World War . . . as the people of this country united in unquestioning devotion to a single national cause" (Steiner, 48–49). She heard about the Nazis, the American and British forces landing in Normandy, France, on D-day, June 6, 1944; the liberation of Paris on August 25, 1944; Germany's surrender on May 7, 1945; the dropping of the atomic bombs on Hiroshima, Japan, on August 6, 1945, and on Nagasaki three days later; and Japan's surrender on September 2, 1945, which ended the war. On the home front, she was most likely aware that mothers and other women went off to work while the men were away fighting; thousands began working in factories to produce war supplies.

Once the war was over, young Americans, including Plath, "listened in numbing disbelief to tales of Hitler's nearly successful attempt to exterminate the Jews and learned to live with the realities of Cold War and atomic capability" (Steiner, 49).

When Plath went off to college in the fall of 1950, there was a lot of tension in America because two opposing political ideologies, democracy and communism, led by the United States and the Soviet Union, struggled for world supremacy. The Soviet Union, a communist state opposed to democracy, seized control of most of the countries in Eastern Europe. In China, Mao Zedong led a communist revolution and took control of mainland China. The United States, which became the greatest world power after World War II, defended non-communist states and worked to stop the domination of the world by communists. This struggle between the American-led democracy and the communist nations became known as the Cold War.

The Korean War began just before Plath started college, when Communist North Korea, supported by the

Soviet Union, invaded South Korea on June 25, 1950. Plath did not approve of the war, writing in 1951 when she was a first-year student at Smith College, "Why do we send the pride of our young men overseas to be massacred for three dirty miles of nothing but earth? Korea was never divided into 'North' and 'South.' They are one people; and our democracy is of no use to those who have not been educated to it. Freedom is not of use to those who do not know how to employ it" (*Unabridged Journals*, 46). Although Dwight D. Eisenhower, elected president in 1952, arranged a cease-fire on July 27, 1953, neither side was able to claim victory.

While the Korean War was going on, Senator Joseph McCarthy played to Americans' fears of communism with a witch hunt to locate and eliminate suspected communists who lived in America. This movement to weed out enemies to America became known by the term *McCarthyism* in early 1950. With extravagant, unsubstantiated accusations, McCarthy, along with "a broad coalition of politicians, bureaucrats, and other anticommunist activists hounded an entire generation of radicals and their associates, destroying lives, careers, and all the institutions that offered a left-wing alternative to mainstream politics and culture" (Schrecker, xii).

Two people arrested as Soviet spies at this time were Julius and Ethel Rosenberg. Tried and found guilty of espionage, they were executed by electric chair in 1953. Their trial and execution were highly controversial. Although some Americans believed that the Rosenbergs were fairly punished because they were dangerous communist spies, others thought their punishments were too harsh for their crimes. Still others, believing that their guilt was debatable, considered them innocent victims. Plath, as evidenced in *The Bell Jar* and her journals, was troubled by their deaths, upset that "nobody very much thinks about how big a human life is, with all the nerves

SENATOR JOSEPH MCCARTHY (PICTURED SPEAKING) LED WHAT MANY DEEMED A "WITCH HUNT" TO IDENTIFY AND CRIMINALIZE SUSPECTED COMMUNISTS LIVING IN AMERICA, DESPITE THE RIGHT GIVEN TO EVERYONE BY THE FIRST AMENDMENT TO FREELY EXPRESS HIS OR HER VIEWS, POLITICAL OR OTHERWISE.

and sinews and reactions and responses that it took centuries and centuries to evolve" (*Unabridged Journals*, 541). In late 1954, the Senate censured McCarthy for making unsupported claims about the number of communists and spies in government, colleges, Hollywood, and elsewhere. From then on, investigations into people alleged to be subversive were carried out more rationally.

Although the Cold War continued and the Vietnam War escalated, Plath made few remarks about world affairs during the 1960s. There are no journal entries for May 5, 1961, when astronaut Alan B. Shepard Jr. became the first American to travel in space. Nor are there any printed journal records at the time of the Cuban missile crisis, a showdown between the United States and the Soviet Union that occurred during the fall of 1962, when Plath was struggling to survive after her husband had left her. When the Soviets sent ships loaded with equipment to set up nuclear missile-launching sites in Fidel Castro's Cuba, President John F. Kennedy, to stop the flow of nuclear arms, sent American ships to blockade neighboring Cuba on October 22, 1962. Nuclear war was prevented when the Soviet ships turned back. As communists and non-communists fought to control South Vietnam, hundreds of thousands of American troops were drafted in the 1960s to fight in the Vietnam War. Though the war started while she was still in college, Plath did not write much about it, only noting that news of fighting "breaks in grimly" (*Unabridged Journals*, 419).

It was the American domestic life that was particularly troubling to Plath. Post–World War II Americans were rather complacent as they lived good lives due to a thriving economy, booming factories and businesses, and widespread prosperity. They were also freed from many deadly diseases. One huge advance in the medical field was a vaccine for poliomyelitis. In 1953, Jonas Salk began his trial vaccines. Found effective, it became the chief weapon against this crippling disease in 1955.

Of great importance to Plath were the treatments for mental diseases. In the 1950s, there were four primary methods of treatment: psychoanalysis, or talk therapy; drug therapy; shock therapy; and psychosurgery or lobotomy. According to psychiatrist Maureen Empfield, throughout the 1950s, most therapists believed that psychoanalytic therapy based on the theories of Sigmund Freud was "the best, if not the only, way to treat mental disorders"; however, present-day therapists find this type of treatment to be of little help to severely depressed people (120). Plath's doctors used psychoanalysis to try to treat her. The second type of treatment, drug therapy, was just beginning when Plath had her first breakdown. In the early part of this decade, the first medicine for mental illness, Thorazine, was developed to help treat schizophrenia (Empfield 151). The third type of treatment, shock therapy, was used for patients with serious mental illnesses. In the 1930s and 1940s, two treatment types were used: insulin shock therapy and electroconvulsive therapy, also called electric shock treatment. Although most American doctors have used electroconvulsive therapy almost exclusively since 1950 (Berger, 349–350), Plath's doctors used both types of shock therapies on her in 1953.

Most hurtful to Plath was the electric shock treatment in which an electric current passes through the patient's brain and produces convulsions or seizures. Luckily, the fourth therapy, psychosurgery or lobotomy, was not used on Plath. For this treatment, doctors operate on the brain to try to alter moods, a dangerous surgery that can have serious, irreversible side effects, including mental retardation. This was evidenced by President Kennedy's family. Seeking to stop the violent moods of mildly retarded Rosemary, the future president's sister, the Kennedys decided that she needed a lobotomy, an operation that "ended her wild moods [and] altered the rest of her personality too," causing her to function at a childlike level (Collier and Horowitz, 116).

With a relatively easy life, the majority of Americans were conformists who willingly followed the societal expectations of desiring a stable family life. Consequently, they married, produced a generation of babies who would later be known as the baby boomers, and built nice homes

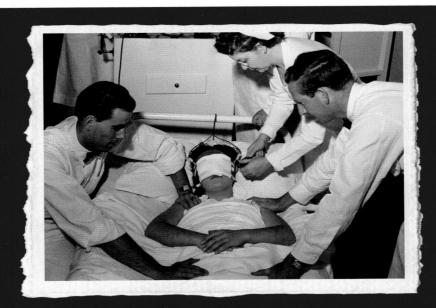

ELECTRIC SHOCK THERAPY WAS A PAINFUL TREATMENT USED PRIMARILY FOR DEPRESSION. IT FIRST BECAME POPULAR—MOSTLY FOR USE ON FEMALE PATIENTS—DURING THE 1940S AND 1950S. ITS USE PLAYS A BIG PART IN *THE BELL JAR*.

on the fringes of the cities, starting suburban living. The men were expected to provide for their families, while the women were supposed to marry, stay at home, raise children, perform housework, and do volunteer work in the community. During the 1950s, according to Plath scholar Linda Wagner-Martin, "the pressure on women to marry—no matter how career oriented, how ambitious, how intelligent—was inescapable" and, therefore, "there were few achieving women during that decade" (*A Novel of the Fifties*, 3).

According to Plath's college roommate, even the well-educated, intelligent "stereotyped Smith girl of the mid

1950's was a conformist" (Steiner, 50) who believed in domestic roles for women. She reports that their graduating class "loved" Governor Adlai Stevenson's "eloquent" commencement address "even if it seemed to hurl us back to the satellite role we had escaped for four years—second-class citizens in a man's world where our only possible achievement was a vicarious one" (Steiner, 109). She says that the governor told them that "our unanimous vocation . . . was to be wives and mothers— thoughtful, discriminating wives and mothers who would use what we had learned in government and history and sociology courses to influence our husbands and children in the direction of rationality" (Steiner, 108–109). The pressure to marry and never have a career plagued and angered Plath, as evidenced in her letters and journals, for, although she wanted to marry and have children, she also yearned to be a successful writer.

By the early 1960s, women were campaigning for equality. Two were especially influential in bringing the difficulties of women to light. One was Gloria Steinem. In an article published in *Esquire* magazine in 1962, she criticized the limitations placed on women because they had to choose between a career and marriage. She later founded the feminist magazine *Ms.* The other activist was Betty Friedan; in *The Feminine Mystique*, published in 1963, she attacked society for treating women as second-class citizens. Under the leadership of these two women, the women's rights movement began. The movement worked for strict enforcement of laws to promote equality for women. Feminists also advocated measures that would aid in equality, such as better child-care facilities so that mothers would be free to work outside the home, legalization of abortion so that women would be free to decide if they wanted to be mothers, and equal pay for equal work (Epstein, 320). Tragically, Plath's life ended when this movement was just starting.

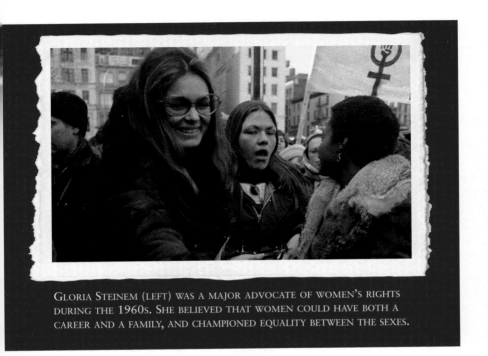

GLORIA STEINEM (LEFT) WAS A MAJOR ADVOCATE OF WOMEN'S RIGHTS DURING THE 1960S. SHE BELIEVED THAT WOMEN COULD HAVE BOTH A CAREER AND A FAMILY, AND CHAMPIONED EQUALITY BETWEEN THE SEXES.

Plath and many other authors in postwar America were disillusioned with American life. The antihero—a failure, rebel, or victim—was popular in American fiction, beginning with Arthur Miller's *Death of a Salesman* in 1949 and J. D. Salinger's *The Catcher in the Rye* in 1951. Lonely, disappointed nonconformists were the subjects of many 1950s novels by Jewish-American writers such as Saul Bellow, Bernard Malamud, and Philip Roth; African-American authors such as Ralph Ellison and James Baldwin; and Caucasian novelists such as Norman Mailer and John Updike. In poetry, Allen Ginsberg was writing "beat" poems to protest conformity. Literary artists of the 1960s, including Alice Walker and Joyce Carol Oates, continued writing about disillusioned people. Plath has become one of the most prominent of these 1960s authors, famous for her poetry and *The Bell Jar*.

THE BELL JAR IS ONE OF PLATH'S MOST FAMOUS WORKS. IT IS A
COMING-OF-AGE STORY THAT REFLECTS EVENTS IN PLATH'S OWN LIFE,
SUCH AS HER INTERNSHIP WITH A MAGAZINE AND HER STRUGGLE
WITH DEPRESSION.

Chapter 3

The Bell Jar

SET IN 1953, *The Bell Jar* is the story of a nineteen-year-old who experiences a nervous breakdown and then begins to recover. Esther Greenwood narrates her own story with candor, insight, and courage, not only painting a vivid picture of insanity, but also revealing her anger at the rigid roles women are expected to play in a society she distrusts.

Plot

Esther, a college student from Massachusetts, is in New York City during a sultry summer, having won a one-month paid internship at a magazine called *Ladies Day*. Along with eleven other girls who are also contest winners, Esther lives at the Amazon Hotel and spends her time working for the magazine and attending gala events the magazine has arranged for them. She is friendly with two other interns—Doreen, a flamboyant, cynical, platinum blonde partygoer who does not take her work seriously, and Betsy, a cheerful, optimistic, wholesome girl from Kansas. Although Esther knows she is "supposed to be having the time of [her] life" (*The Bell Jar*, 2), she feels lifeless and frets about the execution of Julius and Ethel Rosenberg.

On the night she and Doreen get picked up by a local disc jockey, Lenny Shepherd, Esther invents a protective identity, calling herself Elly Higginbottom. After a night of drinking, Esther/Elly leaves Lenny and Doreen, who are jitterbugging and kissing, and walks back to the hotel alone. Hours later, she is awakened when Doreen arrives outside her hotel door, drunk, and collapses in her own vomit.

The next day, Esther meets with her boss, Jay Cee, who scolds her for being indecisive about her future plans. Then Esther goes with Betsy and most of the other girls to an elaborate luncheon. By afternoon, all of the interns except Doreen, who did not attend the banquet, are sick with food poisoning.

When Esther meets Constantin, an interpreter at the United Nations, she decides to let him seduce her. She is disillusioned with her former boyfriend, Buddy Willard. Buddy is a handsome Yale medical student, but Esther regards him as a hypocrite because he had an affair while dating Esther, and still expects Esther to remain a virgin until they are married. Her seduction plans do not work, however, because both Constantin and Esther are so tired that they fall asleep in his apartment.

Back in her hotel room, Esther reminisces about Buddy's courtship, remembering the gruesome hospital tour he gave her of cadavers being dissected, pickled premature babies, anemia victims, and a painful birthing. She also mulls over other times with him: the night he exposed himself to her; the time he boasted about his summer affair with a waitress; the ski trip where she broke her leg; her visits to him at a sanatorium where he was recovering from tuberculosis; and the time he proposed to her and she rejected him.

On her last night in New York, Esther is on a blind date arranged by Doreen. Marco, a woman hater, knocks her down in the mud and nearly rapes her. Before she leaves, he smears her face with the blood from his bloody nose. When she returns to her hotel, she goes to the roof and throws all her clothes away.

Back in Boston, Esther is devastated when she finds out that she has not been accepted into a writing course at Harvard and will, therefore, spend the rest of the summer at home. Although she makes plans to learn shorthand, write a novel, and study for her senior thesis, she grows more and more depressed, becoming unable to sleep, read, or write. She even decides to stop bathing. Her mother tries to help by taking her to a male psychiatrist, Doctor Gordon, who terrifies Esther with electric shock therapy. Not wanting to live, she decides to kill herself. First she thinks she will cut her wrists, but she can only make herself cut her leg. Then she decides to hang herself, but she can't find a place to tie the rope. Next, she resolves to drown herself, but her body keeps floating to the surface. Finally, she takes a huge number of pills and conceals herself in the basement crawl space of her house.

When she wakes up days later, Esther is in a hospital. Once her physical wounds heal, she is sent to the psychological ward of the city hospital, where she is hostile and unreasonable. Due to the generosity of Philomena Guinea, Esther's college scholarship donor, Esther is soon transferred to a private hospital, Belsize, where she is treated by an accomplished woman psychiatrist, Doctor Nolan. With talk therapy, insulin shots, and properly administered electric shock treatments, Esther begins to get well. Another Smith student, Joan, is also at Belsize, and the two become friends. However, Esther is revolted when Joan makes a sexual pass at her.

As she improves, Esther is allowed to leave the hospital for short periods of time. Now using birth control, which gives her the freedom to explore her sexuality, Esther loses her virginity to a Harvard math professor, but the sex causes her to hemorrhage, and she has to go to the emergency room. Soon after this, Joan hangs herself.

By January, Esther is ready to leave the hospital. Although Buddy visits her, both realize that their romance is over. Buddy wonders whether any man will want to marry Esther since she has had a nervous breakdown. As Esther prepares to return to college, she realizes that she is still mentally fragile, and she knows that insanity could one day engulf her again. But she goes out into the world "patched, retreaded and approved for the road" (244).

Themes and Issues

The Search for Identity

Esther Greenwood's search for an authentic identity rather than a socially pleasing façade is the primary theme of *The Bell Jar*, an unconventional story of a young woman coming of age. Critic Tim Kendall calls it "a novel about the searching for and shedding of identity" (53), while scholar Marjorie G. Perloff describes it as the story of a "young American girl's quest to forge her own identity, to be herself rather than what others expect her to be" (509). She claims that "the central action of *The Bell Jar* may be described as the attempt to heal the fracture between inner self and false-self system so that a real and viable identity can come into existence" (509). Plath's heroine does not follow the usual methods of achieving success by either marrying well or establishing an exciting career, but instead by questioning and ultimately rejecting conventional modes of femininity.

At the beginning of the novel, Esther tries to conform to societal expectations. In order to gain approval, she creates a false identity, a common human action, according to psychoanalyst R. D. Laing, who writes that everyone "in some measure wears a mask" (95). From the beginning of the novel, it is clear that the Esther seen by people is a made-up person. In the past, Esther, a people-pleaser, has molded herself to fit others' expectations of her. For her mother, she has been the perfect daughter who had "given her no trouble whatsoever" (202). For her physics teacher, Mr. Manzi, she is the model student, even though she privately reveals that "physics made [her] sick the whole time [she] learned it" (35). For Buddy Willard, she is the idyllic submissive girlfriend who concurs with

In *The Bell Jar*, Esther Greenwood struggles to break away from the expectations of women in a prefeminist age. Esther sees that American women living conventional lives are restricted and trapped in stifling roles.

everything he says, such as falsely agreeing with him when he calls a poem "A piece of dust" (56), and calmly allowing him to expose himself when he thinks she should see his anatomy (68).

When the novel opens, Esther continues to wear a mask. When she is with respectable Betsy, she acts like a well-mannered professional, even though she devours Betsy's share of the caviar as well as her own by keeping the caviar bowl out of Betsy's reach. When she is with naughty Doreen, she appears to be an adventurous sexpot willing to get picked up by a stranger in New York, an action that causes her so much discomfort that she invents a new identity for herself, Elly Higginbottom. The last time she goes out with Doreen and is nearly raped by Marco, she is so disillusioned that she decides to shed her false identity, and, in a symbolic gesture, tosses away all of the expensive clothes that she bought for her New York internship.

Part of Esther's problem in developing an appropriate identity is the result of not finding a satisfactory female role model. The two primary choices she faces are to live a domestic life as a wife and mother, or to have a career as a writer. Her mother isn't much help in advising Esther how to live her life because she urges Esther to give up her own ambitions and learn a practical skill so she can become a man's secretary. Furthermore, Esther has seen that when her mother married, she sacrificed her personal ambitions to become a submissive wife, just like the other local married women: Mrs. Willard, Buddy's mother, and Dodo Conway, Esther's Catholic neighbor. Mrs. Willard, so effaced that she is not even given a first name, fritters away her time in worthless tasks, such as spending weeks making a beautiful rug that her family tramples on; while Dodo Conway, mother of six children, seems to be nothing more than a baby-making machine. Both women have sacrificed independence and freedom for dreary domestic lives.

Literary women do not provide attractive alternatives either. Esther does not admire Jay Cee, the successful literary editor at *Ladies Day*, because she is physically unattractive and therefore seems unwomanly even though she is married. Similarly, she is repelled by Philomena Guinea, the successful but "stupid" novelist who writes sentimental soap-opera-type works that are "crammed from beginning to end with long, suspenseful questions" (41). Esther wonders why she attracts "weird old women" who, she says, "All wanted to adopt me in some way, and, for the price of their care and influence, have me resemble them" (220).

Clearly, Esther does not want to follow the normal societal roles of being either a wife and mother or a person with a career and no home life, but, as Kendall notes, "For Esther, the available identities are mutually exclusive" (54). Because she is "torn between conflicting roles—the sweetheart-*Hausfrau*-mother and the 'life of the poet,' . . . Esther finds life inimical" (Moss, 127).

A second part of Esther's search for identity involves finding and marrying the right guy, but this quest is as hard as finding a suitable female role model. She despises most men because she finds them exploiters and hypocrites. The most suitable male, Buddy, is a dominating hypocrite, and the other men are even less desirable: sleazy Lenny, conventional Constantin, woman-hater Marco, and cocky Dr. Gordon. Probably worst of all is Esther's seducer, the math professor, who casually takes Esther to bed, causes her to severely hemorrhage, and seems unconcerned for her welfare.

After her breakdown, Esther recovers by forming a new, authentic identity. Even though, as Perloff points out, "her external situation has not appreciably changed—she has found neither a lover nor her future vocation—. . . now she can view that situation differently" (521). With the help of Dr. Nolan, who is the only commendable woman in Esther's life, Esther learns to be herself. The new Esther no longer wears a mask to please those around her; instead, she dares to show her true self. Therefore, she has the courage to reject Joan's lesbian invitation, and she is able to speak directly to males. She tells the math professor, "I have a bill here, Irwin" (241), as she makes him pay for her emergency hospitalization, which is a result of their intercourse. She also informs Buddy, who thinks he may have been the cause of both Esther and Joan's insanity, "You had nothing to do with us" (240). By the end of the novel, Esther has realized her need to be a separate human being, independent of others. As Perloff says, "Only when Esther recognizes that she will never be a Jody, a Jay Cee, a Doreen, or a Mrs. Guinea, that she will never marry a Buddy Willard, a Constantin, or a Dr. Gordon, that she wants no lesbian affairs with a Joan or a Dee Dee—does the bell jar lift. . . . [She becomes] an authentic, indeed an exemplary heroine" (521–522).

The Inferior Position of Women

Although *The Bell Jar* was written before the rise of the feminist movement in America, it deals with an important feminist issue: how a woman can become an autonomous person in a world that values her only as an extension of a male. Critic Marilyn Boyer explains that "Plath was assessing the plight of the young woman artist at mid-century who was attempting to overcome the values of domesticity", which was "the mindset prevalent in those times: women should stay at home, cook meals, clean house, and bear children" (200). Vance Bourjaily agrees, stating that Plath is "repudiating the double-dealing by means of which society is stacked against talented, independent women" (138). Although this theme is related to the inferior position of women in the 1950s, it is still relevant because it deals with "the female situation in particular and the human condition in general" (Yalom, 2) by showing the problems encountered by any talented, intelligent person who is placed in an inferior position and yet can neither accept nor reject societal expectations.

From the first chapter, Plath makes it clear that women have limited opportunities to live fulfilling lives. She places the twelve accomplished female interns in the hotel Amazon, a name linked with the powerful Amazon female warriors of Greek mythology who created a nation exclusively of women and lived independent lives. In Plath's novel, however, the women are not free. They are imprisoned in a hotel that is "for women only," a hotel set up to protect the virginity of upper- and middle-class girls; Esther describes them as "mostly girls [her] age with wealthy parents who wanted to be sure their daughters would be living where men couldn't get at them and deceive them" (4). She also notes that the "bored" girls are all waiting to serve men; after attending "posh secretarial schools," they hope to become "secretaries to executives and junior executives," or they are "simply hanging around in New York waiting to get married to some career man or other" (4). Esther loathes these girls with limited ambitions because she "hated the idea of serving men in any way" (76).

Contrary to Esther's sentiments, most males and females expect women to be helpmates of men. Buddy, trying to prove that women should not have independent ambitions, quotes his mother: "What a man wants is a mate and what a woman wants is infinite security," and, "What a man is is an arrow into the future and what a woman is is the place the arrow shoots off from" (72). But Esther, wanting her own career, declares emphatically, "The last thing I wanted was infinite security and to be the place an arrow shoots off from. I wanted change and excitement and to shoot off in all directions myself, like the colored arrow from a Fourth of July rocket" (83).

Not only do men have more career opportunities, they also have greater freedom to fulfill themselves emotionally, especially through sexual activity outside of marriage. Esther analyzes the unfairness of this situation when she reads an article sent to her by her mother. Written by a married female lawyer, "In Defense of Chastity" advances the idea "that a man's world is different from a woman's world and a man's emotions are different from a woman's emotions. . . . the best men wanted to be pure for their wives, and even if they weren't pure, they wanted to be the ones to teach their wives about sex" (81). Esther rebels against this philosophy: "I couldn't stand the idea of a woman having to have a single pure life and a man being able to have a double life, one pure and one not" (81). Wanting the same sexual freedom as men, she later tells Dr. Nolan, "What I hate is the thought of being under a man's thumb. . . . A man doesn't have a worry in the world, while I've got a baby hanging over my head like a big stick, to keep me in line" (221). When she gets fitted for a diaphragm, she is elated, thinking, "I am climbing to freedom, freedom from fear, freedom from marrying the wrong person . . . just because of sex" (223).

Although women are expected to marry, Esther recognizes that marriage leads to a loss of freedom and resists it as a "dreary and wasted life for a girl with fifteen years of straight A's" (84). She knows that what a man "secretly wanted when the wedding service ended was for [his wife] to flatten out underneath his feet like Mrs. Willard's kitchen mat" (85) and spend her time cooking, cleaning, and serving him. Esther reflects on her own educated, talented mother's experience: "Hadn't my own mother told me that as soon as she and my father left Reno on their honeymoon . . . my father said to her, 'Whew, that's a relief, now we can stop pretending and be ourselves'?—and from that day on my mother never had a minute's peace" (85). She also knows that Buddy expects her to give up her own ambitions if she marries him because he had remarked that after she had children she would no longer want to write poetry. Esther, therefore, feels "that when you were married and had children it was like being brainwashed, and afterward you went about numb as a slave in some private, totalitarian state" (85).

Even though societal expectations for women do not change by the end of the novel, Esther is able to rise above the limited roles set for women by managing to integrate a career with a domestic life. After all, the novel is narrated by a woman who is also a wife and mother, who cuts "the plastic starfish off the sun-glasses case for the baby to play with" (3).

Problems of Receiving Good Medical Care

Esther is continually bothered by what she sees as the arrogance and insensitivity of male medical doctors. She first mentions this when she witnesses the excruciating pain of a drugged woman giving birth while the insensitive male doctors are oblivious to her suffering. Near the end of the novel, when Esther is hemorrhaging, the male doctors again act with indifference. Joan has to call five doctors before one will help Esther; the rest are too busy pursuing weekend pleasures.

Psychiatric medicine particularly comes under fire in this novel. Esther finds Dr. Gordon "conceited" (129) and unhelpful. Unconcerned with her true state of mental health, he refuses to listen to her, addresses her mother instead of her, and gives her pat answers. His mistreatment of her by his poorly administered electric shock treatments leads her into greater depression and results in a suicide attempt. Joan also tells about the unsympathetic attitude of male psychiatrists. Both women seem to do better with female psychiatrists.

In spite of Esther's recovery, the types of treatments used to cure mental illness are questionable. Particularly dubious is the surgical procedure called lobotomy, which was performed on Valerie; although it eliminates her anger, it also robs her of all emotions. Shock therapy, which is successfully used on Esther, erases negative images in her mind so that she can return to normalcy, but one of its possible side effects is a dulling of intelligence. The final success of all methods comes under question because Joan, who seems to be cured, kills herself.

Analysis

Structure

The novel is divided into three primary sections based on setting and topic. The first, chapters one through nine, takes place in New York where Esther interns for a fashion magazine. It introduces the main characters and suggests the major conflicts in a number of episodes: a night out with Doreen, who spends much of the time with Lenny and returns to the hotel drunk; food poisoning from an elaborate luncheon; a date with a United Nations simultaneous interpreter and her attempted seduction of him; and a near rape by Marco. Intermingled with the New York scenes are flashbacks to her unsatisfactory romance with Buddy Willard. This part ends with Esther discarding the expensive clothes she purchased for this trip. Throughout these chapters, Esther is seen as depressed and at odds with society. She forms two identities—Esther, the socially good girl, and Elly, the disreputable flirt.

The second section, chapters ten through thirteen, takes place in Esther's hometown of Boston. The chapters describe Esther's descent into depression. During her weeks at home, she has been seen by Dr. Gordon, a psychiatrist who botches electric shock therapy. So miserable that she mostly regards herself as Elly, Esther attempts to kill herself by cutting, hanging, drowning, and finally taking sleeping pills. These chapters show the horrors of a depression that has become so deep that a person does not want to live.

The story of Esther's recovery from depression, chapters fourteen through twenty, comprises the third section. It takes place in hospitals, where Esther is treated with talk therapy, insulin, and electric shock therapy. The book ends as Esther tenuously makes her way into the world with the fear that she may relapse as Joan did.

Narrative Voice

Everything is seen through the eyes of Esther Greenwood, who tells the story of a time in her youth when she suffered a nervous breakdown. Plath adopts a first person narrative style that helps show Esther's disorientation by using a voice "constructed to be abnormal, unreliable," jumping "between objective statements and her own reaction to them" and thus forcing the reader "to fuse two kinds of information—factual information, about the external events of this period, and subjective information, about the protagonist's state of mind" (Wagner-Martin, *A Novel of the Fifties*, 25–26). Since Esther is extremely depressed, some of her impressions are incorrect, but her view of society as being basically oppressive to women is accurate.

Characters

Esther Greenwood

"An academically brilliant, socially insecure, and constantly introspective college junior" (Bourjaily, 135), Esther is unable to fit into any of the acceptable roles defined by her society because she wants to be both an independent woman with a career as a professor, writer, or scholar, and also a wife and mother. She dislikes those who have followed only one path: the strong, successful, professional females and the feminine, domestic women. As she spends the month of June in New York City, she becomes increasingly worried about her future. Her anxiety leads to such a severe depression that she attempts to kill herself. With the help of a psychiatrist, she recovers by learning to be an independent person secure in her own feelings. Wagner-Martin points out that, by the end of the novel, Esther is "a much more confident person. She knows she does not want to be like the lobotomized Valerie, incapable of any emotion. She feels real grief at Joan's funeral, and real anger at Buddy's condescending visit. She understands the rejection implicit in her mother's refusal to accept the truth about her illness, and the corresponding and somewhat compensatory generosity of Dr. Nolan's acceptance of it" (42). When she leaves the hospital, Esther declares, "I was my own woman" (223).

The Interns: Doreen and Betsy

Plath uses a number of double characters to show alternate choices possible for Esther.

Betsy and Doreen, Esther's fellow interns, pull her in opposite directions. Good, respectable Betsy, nicknamed "Pollyanna Cowgirl" by Doreen, represents the side of Esther that wants to conform to society. Doreen, a sexy, adventurous southerner, represents her other side—the young woman who wants to be sophisticated, socially knowledgeable, and unrepressed by societal expectations. While she is in New York, Esther wavers between these two friends, confessing, "I wondered why I couldn't go the whole way doing what I should any more [like Betsy]. This made me sad and tired. Then I wondered why I couldn't go the whole way doing what I shouldn't, the way Doreen did, and this made me even sadder and more tired" (30). Esther is unable to reconcile these two aspects of herself until the end of the novel.

Joan Gilling

Esther regards Joan Gilling, a girl from her hometown, as "the beaming double of my old best self" (205). Like Esther, Joan is a Smith student, a former girlfriend of Buddy Willard, and a patient at the psychiatric hospital.

Psychologically, they are also alike, being unconventional overachievers who, nevertheless, think they should emulate Mrs. Willard, whom society regards as the ideal wife. In their confusion over their roles as women, both attempt suicide and later defy sexual norms for women, Joan by becoming a lesbian and Esther by engaging in premarital sex. After a short recovery time, Joan leaves the hospital but kills herself soon after. When Esther attends Joan's funeral, she affirms her own selfhood.

Mrs. Greenwood

Esther's mother has followed the traditional role for women by marrying and raising a family, and has, therefore, disregarded "the possibility of personal distinction for a woman" (Aird, 91). Hardworking and well-meaning, Mrs. Greenwood gave up her own writing ambitions to serve her husband and, after he died, to support her children by teaching shorthand and typing, a job she "secretly . . . hated" (39). In spite of her mother's self-sacrifice, Esther declares that she hates her mother because she pressures Esther to conform to societal expectations. In particular, Esther resents her mother for encouraging her to learn shorthand so she can be a secretary who is "in demand among all the up-and-coming young men . . . transcrib[ing] letter after thrilling letter" (76), and for looking upon Buddy Willard as a desirable mate, even though he would squelch Esther's individuality. Furthermore, Esther is angry that her mother seems more concerned about the social consequences of her breakdown than about her health. Because Mrs. Greenwood advocates conformity, this talented, highly educated woman provides an inadequate role model for ambitious Esther.

Buddy Willard

Although Buddy Willard is regarded by most of society as the perfect mate, to Esther he is like the other young males, Lenny Shepherd, Constantin, Marco, Cal, and Irwin—chauvinistic, insensitive, and domineering. A controlling, arrogant male who uses his knowledge of science to dominate Esther, he shows off by taking her on a tour of the university hospital, an experience that leaves Esther disillusioned. As Buddy tries to further educate Esther by revealing himself, she remains unemotional, regarding his body as "turkey neck and turkey gizzards" (69). Besides being arrogant, he is also possessive. A typical mid-century male who regards a woman as his property, Buddy seems pleased that Esther will be in a cast for months after she breaks her leg, thus ensuring that she will be unable to date others while he is hospitalized for tuberculosis.

Symbols
Symbols are tangible items such as objects or people that stand for abstract ideas or thoughts. In *The Bell Jar*, they show Esther's inner, subjective world.

The Bell Jar
The major symbol of the novel is the bell jar, a glass used to enclose something. In science, it is an inverted glass jar used to isolate and display an unusual object; in the home, it is a container used by housewives to can fruits or vegetables. Plath uses it to show confinement, alienation, and insanity. Just as a bell jar is used to separate a specimen from all other things, Esther, disconnected from everyone and cut off from normal human experience, is isolated inside an airless jar where she says she is "stewing in [her] own sour air" (185). There is nothing she can do to escape because, she says, "The air of the bell jar wadded round me and I couldn't stir" (186). It is only after she has been given correctly managed electric shock treatments that she is able to break out of the sick, confining space of the bell jar. But even then, it threatens to enclose her again, for she sees that "the bell jar hung, suspended, a few feet above my head" (215). When she is pronounced sane, she wonders if

THE FIG TREE IS A RECURRING SYMBOL IN *THE BELL JAR*. FIG TREES
ARE FEATURED IN RELIGIOUS TEXTS, INCLUDING THOSE OF CHRISTIANITY
AND BUDDHISM.

the bell jar will trap her again: "How did I know that someday—at college, in Europe, somewhere, anywhere—the bell jar, with its stifling distortions, wouldn't descend again?" (241).

Plath also uses the bell jar to describe the way all women are confined, trapped in suffocating lives. Esther observes that "girls playing bridge and gossiping and studying in the college to which I would return . . . sat under bell jars of a sort" (238). Plath seems to be saying that American women living conventional lives are all restricted. The bell jar of societal conformity keeps women restrained and limited.

The Fig Tree

The fig tree is used twice in the novel to show Esther's disillusionment with marriage partners and with life choices for females. It is introduced when she reads the story of a

Los Angeles Times PICTORIAL

VOL. LXXII | IN THREE PARTS ★★★ | SATURDAY MORNING, JUNE 20, 1953 | 42 PAGES | DAILY, 10¢

ROSENBERGS DIE

Pair Executed for Atom Spying

END OF TRAIL—Summons to death in electric chair came swiftly for Atom Spies Ethel and Julius Rosenberg after stay was revoked and clemency was refused.

Supreme Court and Eisenhower Reject Couple's Last Pleas

OSSINING, N.Y., June 19—Atom Spies Julius and Ethel Rosenberg died in Sing Sing Prison's electric chair shortly before sundown today. The executions followed quickly after the Supreme Court set aside a stay of execution granted Wednesday by Justice William O. Douglas and President Eisenhower's refusal to grant them clemency.

SING SING PRISON, N.Y., June 19 (UP)—Atom Spies Julius and Ethel Rosenberg were ordered electrocuted late today for betraying their country's secrets to Russia and threatening the lives of millions by bringing the world closer to an atomic war.

The Justice Department set the time for the doomed couple's death in Sing Sing Prison's electric chair after a day of suspense in which the U.S. Supreme Court denied their final appeals and President Eisenhower again refused executive clemency.

Warden Wilfred Denno announced first the husband and wife espionage team would be put to death in the gray-walled prison's death chamber "before sundown," which comes at 8:30 p.m. (5:30 PDT) local time at Sing Sing. Later he said the first execution would come at 8 p.m. EDT, with the second a few minutes later.

Spend Time Together

The Jewish Sabbath starts at sundown, and the plans to execute the couple before that time, instead of at the traditional 11 p.m., were announced after the prison rabbi said he would ask the Rosenbergs if they wanted to request a delay until tomorrow night.

The Rosenbergs spent their last afternoon together and then ate a dinner of regular prison fare—hard-boiled

WEST BERLIN'S RED OFFICES WRECKED
Anti-Communist Mob Storms Party Building; Soviets Rush Reinforcements in East Sector

20 Injured as Fireworks Blast Levels Factory

TRUCE DELEGATES FACE CRUCIAL TALK
Reds Demand Session as Communist Radios Charge Connivance by U.S. in POW Escapes

Clouds Clamp Cool Damper as Summer Nears

0068310 ROSENBERG EXECUTION, 1953.
Credit: The Granger Collection, New York

JULIUS AND ETHEL ROSENBERG WERE EXECUTED IN 1953 FOR SHARING INFORMATION ON THE NUCLEAR BOMB WITH THE SOVIET UNION. WOMEN—ESPECIALLY MOTHERS—WERE RARELY GIVEN THE DEATH PENALTY, AND THE ROSENBERGS HAD TWO YOUNG SONS. AMERICANS WERE DIVIDED ON THEIR GUILT—AND THE JUSTICE OF THEIR DEATH SENTENCE.

Jewish man and a beautiful nun who meet and fall in love under a fig tree but then go their separate ways, a tale that reminds her of her dying love for Buddy Willard: "We had met together under our own imaginary fig tree, . . . and then something awful happened and we went our separate ways" (55).

The second time the fig tree is mentioned, Esther sees it as a metaphor for her life choices: "One fig was a husband and a happy home and children, and another fig was a famous poet and another fig was a brilliant professor, and another fig was Ee Gee, the amazing editor, and another fig was Europe and Africa and South America, and another fig was Constantin and Socrates and Attila and a pack of other lovers with queer names and offbeat professions, and another fig was an Olympic lady crew champion, and beyond and above these figs were many more figs I couldn't quite make out" (77). But Esther, unable to choose one because she "wanted each and every one of them, but choosing one meant losing all the rest" (55), starves to death. Through the fig tree image, then, Esther sees that, as a female, any choice she makes means giving up all other ambitions. And if she makes no choice, the figs will rot, leaving nothing to choose.

Electricity

Plath mentions electricity several times in the novel to show how society can use something that is neither good nor bad in itself as a tool of both punishment and help. At first, Esther sees electricity as something terrifying because it hurts people's bodies. As a little girl, she had experienced its destructive power when she moved an old floor lamp, grasping its fuzzy cord. In vivid terms, she describes her terror when she received an electric shock: "Then something leapt out of the lamp in a blue flash and shook me till my teeth rattled, and I tried to pull my hands off, but they were stuck, and I screamed, or a scream was torn from my throat, for I didn't recognize it, but heard it soar and quaver in the air like a violently disembodied spirit" (144). Her terror of electricity is found on the opening page of the novel as Esther thinks about the upcoming electrocution of the Rosenbergs, stating, the "idea of being electrocuted makes me sick. . . . I couldn't help wondering what it would be like, being burned alive, all along your nerves" (1). By the middle of the novel, she knows what electrocution feels like when incompetent Dr. Gordon administers electric shock treatment: "Then something bent down and took hold of me and shook me like the end of the world. Whee-ee-ee-ee-ee, it shrilled, through an air crackling with blue light, and with each flash a great jolt drubbed me till I thought my bones would break and the sap fly out of me like a split plant" (143). Feeling that she is being punished, she "wondered what terrible thing it was that [she] had done" (143).

Understandably, when Esther prepares to receive electric shock therapy from Dr. Nolan, she is once again terrified, looking upon it as an "execution" (211) performed by a "cadaverous" nurse (213). After the electrodes are placed on her temples, Esther bites down on the part inserted in her mouth "in panic" and seems to die: "darkness wiped me out like chalk on a blackboard" (214). But when she awakens, she is "at peace"; with the bell jar raised above her head, she is finally able to breathe fresh air (215). It is electricity, then, that brings Esther back to sanity.

The Rosenbergs

Esther reflects on two real people of the 1950s, Julius and Ethel Rosenberg, the husband and wife electrocuted for being Russian spies. Esther sympathizes with this couple who are, as Wagner-Martin explains, "being violated not only by being killed but by 'being burned along their nerves'. . . because they have broken a cultural rule" (The

Bell Jar: *A Novel of the Fifties*, 29, 23) by becoming traitors to the country. Esther relates to them because she also wants to break the rules of society to live an independent life. Esther, then, wonders what will happen to her if she, like the Rosenbergs, fails to conform to societal conventions.

Mirrors

Plath uses mirrors, which show external reflections or façades of the different Esthers, to help portray Esther's descent into insanity. In the first section of the novel, mirror imagery reveals Esther's disconnection from herself. A split personality, she does not know how to live her life, whether to remain the good, socially acceptable girl or change into a rebellious nonconformist. After walking back from Lenny's from a night spent trying to be like nonconformist Doreen, she does not recognize herself when she first looks at the hotel's mirror. Instead, she "noticed a big-smudgy-eyed Chinese woman staring idiotically into my face. It was only me, of course. I was appalled to see how wrinkled and used up I looked" (18). A few minutes later in her room, her image is still distorted in her "slightly warped" bureau mirror: "The face in it looked like the reflection in a ball of dentist's mercury" (19). After Marco tries to rape Esther, her image looks "*like a sick Indian*" (112).

She is also disconnected from herself because she does not know what career to follow. Thus, when she looks in her compact mirror while getting ready for the magazine's photographer, she says that the "face that peered back at me seemed to be peering from the grating of a prison cell after a prolonged beating. It looked bruised and puffy and all the wrong colors. It was a face that needed soap and water and Christian tolerance" (102).

At home in Boston she becomes more irrational, and thinks of her image as a separate entity. When she is standing in front of her medicine cabinet thinking about cutting her wrists, she realizes that she might be able to go through with her suicide by watching herself in the mirror because, she reasons: "If I looked in the mirror while I did it, it would be like watching somebody else, in a book or a play" (147–148). But she realizes she will not cut her wrists because "the person in the mirror was paralyzed and too stupid to do a thing" (148).

Up to this point, Esther, although she does not initially recognize herself, does eventually understand that the images in the mirrors are hers. But after her near-fatal suicide attempt, she does not know herself at all. When the hospital nurse gives her a mirror, Esther thinks she is looking at the picture of a person so strange that "you couldn't tell whether the person in the picture was a man or a woman, because their hair was shaved off and sprouted in bristly chicken-feather tufts all over their head. One side of the person's face was purple, and bulged out in a shapeless way, shading to green along the edges, and then to a sallow yellow. The person's mouth was pale brown, with a rose-colored sore at either corner" (174). It is only when she smiles and the "mouth in the mirror cracked into a grin" (175) that Esther realizes this deformed stranger is herself. After this, as Esther begins recovering, there are no more mirrors because there are no more reflections of Esther's different façades. The real Esther has now joined her mind and body into one.

Motifs
Motifs are recurring elements that help develop the themes of the novel.

Illness
Plath uses physical and mental illness to show the confining society as sick. Perloff believes that "all illness is to be viewed as part of the same spectrum: disease, whether

mental or physical, is an index to the human inability to cope with an unlivable situation" (520–521). The novel begins with physical illnesses—inebriated Doreen lies in her own vomit; the interns get ptomaine poisoning after eating beautiful avocados stuffed with crabmeat; healthy Buddy has succumbed to tuberculosis and goes to a sanatorium to recover; and Esther breaks her leg skiing. The center of the novel moves from physical sickness to mental illness as Esther suffers a nervous breakdown. At the end of the book, physical illness returns when Esther nearly bleeds to death and Joan hangs herself. All of these incidents relate to possible lifestyles that are open to Esther, and they show that every choice leads to danger and pain. Rebelling against societal norms as drunken Doreen does is repellant, while conforming to society like Betsy results in food poisoning. Dating a marriageable man leads to a painful broken leg for Esther when Buddy arrogantly tries to teach her to ski. Her first sexual experience, which she thinks will open up the mysteries of life and place her on an equal level with males, results in such heavy bleeding that she needs to go to the hospital. And becoming "sane" like Joan causes so much unhappiness that death is better. These numerous instances of illness point out that, for women, it is very difficult to live wholesome or fulfilling lives because traditional lifestyles often lead to suffering and even death. Esther, therefore, needs to find a new way to live.

Death

Images of death reflect Esther's lifeless existence. From the first page of her novel, Esther views her life as dead: "It was like the first time I saw a cadaver. For weeks afterward, the cadaver's head—or what there was left of it—floated up behind my eggs and bacon at breakfast and behind the face of Buddy Willard, who was responsible for my seeing it in the first place, and pretty soon I felt as though I were carrying that cadaver's head around with me on a string, like some black, noseless balloon stinking of vinegar" (1–2). Cadavers and pickled fetuses haunt Esther throughout the first section of the novel. At the end of this section, as Esther stands on the hotel rooftop, she sees her clothes, symbols of her professional life, as cremated bodies, describing them as falling "flutteringly, like a loved one's ashes" (111).

In the second section of the novel, Esther thinks about death more and more frequently, and her main preoccupation is how to kill herself. However, as she recovers in the third section, she thinks less about death. In fact, when Joan kills herself, Esther, now ready to face the world, does not concentrate on death but on life, as her heart pounds out, "I am, I am, I am" (243).

Literary Reception

When *The Bell Jar* was first published in England in January 1963 under the pseudonym Victoria Lucas, the book was not widely reviewed, but three early reviews were mostly positive. The novel was favorably compared to the wildly popular novel by J. D. Salinger, *The Catcher in the Rye*, as a "clever first novel . . . the first feminine novel . . . in the Salinger mood." Other reviews proclaimed it "a brilliant and moving book" that excelled in "both language and characterization" and praised it as "astonishingly skillful," "honest," "intensely interesting," "brave," and "terribly likeable." However, one reviewer qualified his endorsement of Plath's book, stating that the author "can certainly write," but adding that "if she can learn to shape as well as she imagines, she may write an extremely good book."

After Plath's suicide in 1963 and the publication of *Ariel* in 1965, the general public and critics became extremely interested in her works and life. They sympathized with her plight, regarding her as a victim of a confining society and an unfaithful husband. As a result of Plath's fame, critical emphasis changed from analysis to biographical comparisons. Thus, by the time *The Bell Jar* was published again in Britain in 1967 under Plath's name, reviewers either looked at parallels between the novel and Plath's life or compared the book to the *Ariel* poems. *The Bell Jar* was admired for its "notable honesty" about Plath's mental states and its "fierce clarity so terrifying in the great poems in *Ariel*."

By the time the novel appeared in America in 1971, Plath, idolized as a woman trapped by society and driven to suicide, had become nearly a household name, and Plath groupies had formed clubs (McCullough, xiv). Many American critics looked at the book as autobiographical, feeling that "it's impossible to read *The Bell Jar* [without] the knowledge of Sylvia Plath's doom color[ing] its pages." However, a few recognized the book's intrinsic value, finding that it is filled with "wit and agony" and "represents recognizable experience." Comparisons to Salinger's popular neurotic characters continued, as critics proclaimed it "a fine novel, as bitter and remorseless as [Plath's] last poems—the kind of book Salinger's Franny might have written about herself ten years later, if she had spent those ten years in Hell."

Immediately, *The Bell Jar* became an extremely popular book in America. Frances McCullough, an editor at *Harper's*, lists a number of social factors in America that contributed to its success: first, the women's movement was in full swing; second, confessional literature was popular; third, people were interested in new views about death and how to cope with it, especially since the publication of Elisabeth Kübler-Ross's book on death and Erich Segal's poignant *Love Story*; and fourth, people were fascinated with depression and mental illness, and particularly with Sylvia Plath, who was Exhibit A in A. Alvarez's romantic book about suicide, *The Savage God: A Study of*

Suicide, published in 1971 (xiv). As a result, *The Bell Jar* became an immediate best seller and was named one of *Book World*'s "Fifty Notable Books" of 1971 (Wagner-Martin, *A Novel of the Fifties*, 13).

In the decades since its publication in the United States, the novel has remained extremely popular because its topics continue to be relevant. Depression has become widely acknowledged in America, and although Plath's type of nervous breakdown was never diagnosed, her frank descriptions of schizophrenic views remain unequalled by other writers. And suicide continues to fascinate people. *The Bell Jar* is regarded as an important book in the study of mental illness, a "frightening" book about suicide, admired because "it bears the stamp of authority. Reading it, we are up against the raw experience of nightmare, not the analysis or understanding of it" (Moss, 129). It is proclaimed to be "perhaps the most compelling and controlled account of a mental breakdown to have appeared in American fiction" (Tanner, 262).

A second topic, women's roles in society, continues to be discussed, not only by feminists but also by all those concerned with social justice. *The Bell Jar* played a major role in bringing this issue to light. In 1972, Patricia Meyer Spacks addressed the novel's issue of women's limited roles in 1950s America: "Female sexuality is the center of horror: babies in glass jars, women bleeding in childbirth, Esther herself thrown in the mud by a sadist, hemorrhaging after her single sexual experience. To be a woman is to bleed and burn. . . . Womanhood is entrapment, escaped from previously by artistic activity, escaped from surely only by death" (quoted in Wagner-Martin, *A Novel of the Fifties*, 11).

Men, such as Mason Harris, agree that the book is an accurate analysis of the "stifling hermetically-sealed world of the Eisenhower 'Fifties'" which "gives an authentic vision of a period which exalted the most oppressive ideal of reason and stability" (54–56). Ellen Moers declared in 1976 that "no writer [had] meant more to the current feminist movement" than Sylvia Plath (xv). A dozen years later Catharine Stimpson reaffirmed this belief, championing Plath's novel as "a vigorous polemic about a 'problem that had no name,' women's inferior position" and declaring that *The Bell Jar*, along with Betty Friedan's *The Feminine Mystique*, helped stimulate the twentieth-century feminist movement (1064). Today, the novel "continues to speak for readers who feel trapped in the social paradigms that culture mandates and lends retrospective light to that period in mid-century America when Plath and her generation were trying to exist as achieving but still-subordinated women" (Wagner-Martin, *A Novel of the Fifties*, 12).

But probably the most important reason for *The Bell Jar*'s continued popularity is that it relates to the personal experiences of young women who, like Esther, have to figure out "how to sort out your life, how to work out what you want, how to deal with men and sex, how to be true to yourself and how to figure out what that means" (McCullough, xvi). Wagner-Martin accurately points out that the "continued steady sales of Plath's novel—not only in the United States and England but throughout the world, translated into countless languages—show implicitly that her themes and characters are not dated, that the narrative *The Bell Jar* presents remains important for readers of the 1990s" (*A Novel of the Fifties*, 9). Based on its unceasing sales and critical analyses, *The Bell Jar* continues to speak to readers in the twenty-first century.

ARIEL

Poems by Sylvia Plath

IN THE 2004 *ARIEL: THE RESTORED EDITION*, PLATH'S POEMS APPEAR THE WAY SHE ARRANGED THEM, RATHER THAN THE ORDER IN WHICH HER HUSBAND, TED HUGHES, HAD ORGANIZED THEM WHEN THEY WERE ORIGINALLY PUBLISHED IN 1965. THIS EDITION INCLUDES A FOREWORD BY PLATH'S DAUGHTER, FRIEDA HUGHES.

Chapter 4

Poetry

DURING HER LIFETIME, Sylvia Plath published one book of poetry, *The Colossus*, first printed in 1960. Before her death in 1963, she had prepared a second one, carefully arranging the order of her poems. This appeared in 1965 as *Ariel*, although the order had been changed and a number of late poems were added. Two additional posthumous volumes were published in 1971: *Crossing the Water*, a book of poems written between *The Colossus* and *Ariel*, and *Winter Trees*, a slim volume containing eighteen late poems and *Three Women*, a play written for BBC radio. Periodically, other poems appeared in small limited editions. In 1981, all of these poems, and others that had never been published, were gathered and chronologically arranged in one volume, *The Collected Poems*, carefully edited by Ted Hughes. Plath's original arrangement of the *Ariel* poems was printed as *Ariel: The Restored Edition* in 2004.

John Frederick Nims writes that Plath employs similar techniques in all of her poems, "the sense of language and of metaphor; the throat-produced sounds of her poetry; the physical rhythms that invigorate it," which give them a "timeless excellence" (138). He considers her "more brilliant at metaphor than others popularly grouped with her as confessional poets" because "almost all of the metaphors are on target" (138, 139). The sounds she creates are seen not only in her careful choice of "distinguished and elegant" words (Nims, 151), but also in her rhymes. Plath's favorite rhyming method is what is termed slant rhyme or off rhyme, words that have similar but not identical endings, such as "vast / compost / must." Many of her poems, particularly in *Ariel*, are grouped into stanzas of three lines, called terza rima, but she does not confine her rhyming words to one stanza. Her rhythmic patterns vary. Sometimes she follows the oldest form of English poetry of having two stresses and any number of unstressed syllables per line; but generally, especially in *Ariel*, she uses the most basic English language rhythm, iambic meter, which is a two-syllable pulsation with the second syllable accented. Using this form makes her poetry very readable because it sounds like common speech. By using these techniques, Plath's poems portray a sense of reality because "what we hear almost everywhere is a real voice in a real body in a real world" (Nims, 152).

Plath's poetry is often included in anthologies. Five of her most popular poems are "Ariel," "The Colossus," "Daddy," "Lady Lazarus," and "Metaphors."

"Ariel" (*Ariel*), 1962

In "Ariel," the title poem in Plath's last written volume of poetry, the female speaker gains a new perception of herself while taking a wild horseback ride one morning. Exhilarated, the rider is able to cast off, to "unpeel" (20) things that trap her or hold her down. With her new sense of freedom, "she takes on all the independence, the aggression, that her culture had attempted to deny her" (Wagner-Martin, *Sylvia Plath*, 220) and becomes both an "arrow" (27)—an active, autonomous person—and "God's lioness" (4)—a warrior for God.

This highly regarded, although often-criticized poem is complicated and ambiguous. The title itself refers to several different things: Plath's horse, a shape-shifting spirit, and a biblical figure. Ariel is, first of all, the name of Plath's horse. As Ted Hughes relates in his "Notes on the Chronological Order of Sylvia Plath's Poems": "ARIEL was the name of the horse on which she went riding weekly. Long before, while she was a student at

Cambridge (England), she went riding with an American friend out towards Grantchester. Her horse bolted, the stirrups fell off, and she came all the way home to the stables, about two miles, at full gallop, hanging around the horse's neck" (194). In the first six stanzas, the poem can be read literally as an early morning horse ride. It begins with the rider mounting the horse and continues as the horse gallops faster and faster until the landscape becomes unrecognizable and the rider is hurled through the air. The last five stanzas, however, move beyond the actual horseback ride into some type of unusual blending of the horse and the rider.

In literature, Ariel is an androgynous spirit that can change sex and shape at any time. Milton, in *Paradise Lost*, names one of the rebel angels Ariel (6:371), while Alexander Pope uses Ariel as Belinda's guardian angel in *The Rape of the Lock*. However, the most well-known literary Ariel is found in Shakespeare's *The Tempest*. This creative spirit controls the wind and waves, lures men with its beautiful singing, and casts spells. Like Shakespeare's Ariel, Plath's rider is a spirit capable of changing shape, first becoming one with the horse, "How one we grow" (5), and then transforming itself into "White / Godiva" (19–20), "foam to wheat" (23), "a glitter of seas" (23), an "arrow" (27), and "dew" (28). By using these associations, Plath's rider transforms herself into "pure, androgynous creative energy" (Britzolakis, 184), like Shakespeare's Ariel.

Although *The Tempest*'s Ariel is a creative spirit, it is also a prisoner, held captive by the magician Prospero. Ariel yearns for liberty, a gift Prospero promises early in the play, telling Ariel, "Thou shalt be as free / As mountain winds" (1.2.502–503), and setting the spirit free in the final act. Comparably, Plath's rider wants liberty and gains freedom with her death as she "flies / Suicidal . . . / Into the red / Eye, the cauldron of morning" (28–31).

This theme of oppression and promised deliverance is also seen in the third way Plath uses the name Ariel by recalling the biblical Ariel, the word used by Isaiah to refer to Jerusalem, a city condemned to trials and troubles: "Yet I will distress Ariel, and there shall be moaning and lamentation, and Jerusalem shall be to me like an Ariel" (Isaiah 29:2). But God also promises to rescue the city: "the multitude of all the nations that fight against Ariel, all that fight against her and her stronghold, and who distress her, shall be like a dream, a vision of the night" (Isaiah 29:7). Scholar Merritt Y. Hughes says that in Hebrew, the word *Ariel* means "lion of God" and is "a kind of epithet of Jerusalem." He also points out that rabbinical scholarship translates the Ariel of Isaiah 29 as "valiant one" and that the name "acquired such meanings as 'hero,' 'champion,' 'mighty warrior,' and 'angel' or 'messenger'" (196; note 371). Clearly, Plath has this biblical meaning in mind, for the rider not only calls herself "God's lioness" (4) but also, as God's valiant hero, becomes an arrow that "absorbs the power of the avenging God" (Uroff, 166). The arrow image reminds readers of conformist Mrs. Willard of *The Bell Jar*, who says that men are arrows and women are the places they shoot off from, a saying Esther Greenwood hates because she wants to be the arrow (*The Bell Jar*, 72). In "Ariel," the woman is the arrow who takes on the active roles society assigned to males. But, in order to be an "arrow," she has to sacrifice things that hold her back, the "child's cry" (24), motherhood and "dead hands, dead stringencies" (21). As an arrow, the speaker finds independence and freedom.

By using these three Ariels, Plath gives her poem multiple levels of meaning. As Caroline King Barnard Hall asserts, "Ariel, then, is poet, rider, and horse; she is a swift, indomitable presence galloping unflinchingly ahead; and she is an androgynous spirit assuming the form of anything or anyone who is oppressed and yearning for freedom. She is God's lioness" (115).

Some critics regard "Ariel" as a great achievement because of Plath's images. For example, Jon Rosenblatt explains that "we see, hear, touch, and taste the process of disintegration: the horse emerging from the darkness of the morning, the sun beginning to rise as Ariel rushes uncontrollably across the countryside, the rider trying to catch the brown neck but instead 'tasting' the blackberries on the side of the road. Then all the rider's perceptions are thrown together: the horse's body and the rider's merge. She . . . flies toward the burning sun that has now risen" (130).

Besides praising Plath's vivid imagery, critics also rave about her techniques, finding that her poem seems to sing. Its music comes from Plath's use of slant rhymes. In almost every three-line stanza, two lines rhyme: "darkness" / "distance" (1, 3), "grow" / "furrow" (5, 6), "arc" / "catch" (8, 9), "dark" / "Hooks" (11, 12), "mouthfuls" / "else" (13, 15), "air" / "hair" (16, 17), "I" / "cry" (22, 24), "Wall" / "Arrow" (25, 27), and "drive" / "red" (29, 30). Plath also uses other musical devices, including internal rhyme, "Pour of tor" (3); alliteration, "cannot catch" (9); and assonance, "heels and knees" (6). The stanza form—ten stanzas of three lines each—parallels the threefold meaning of Ariel: horse, spirit, and God's lioness. The one-line concluding stanza shows total unity as woman/horse/spirit/lioness fling themselves into ultimate freedom by totally abandoning bodies and entities.

Not everyone agrees that "Ariel" is a well-formed, meaningful poem. For example, Judson Jerome, poet and author of *The Poet's Handbook*, does not see it as a great or even a good poem. Although he believes that "Plath was a brilliant, gifted poet," and that "many of her poems . . . are powerful and clear" (191), he does not like "Ariel." He writes: "I am sure there is an explanation of 'Ariel' . . . in some academic critique. But I am also sure the poem makes no sense. One might study it, as a psychiatrist might analyze the doodling of a mental patient for insights into madness, for a better understanding of the woman. But its value as art for any sort of general audience is questionable" (191). He believes that the poem is incoherent because Plath omits transitions to connect her ideas and writes with images, phrases, and individual words instead of forming sentences (191).

However, most critics are not this negative, and, in fact, many regard "Ariel" as Plath's greatest poem. Kathleen Margaret Lant calls it "the work which most perfectly embodies Plath's conflicting sets of figures concerning power and nakedness" (654), while Stanley Plumly pronounces it "Plath's singular and famous example of the form completely at one with its substance" (24). Rosenblatt is even more enthusiastic, calling "Ariel" "Plath's finest single construction" (130).

"The Colossus" (*The Colossus*), 1959

The title poem of Plath's first volume of poetry, "The Colossus," is literally concerned with a gigantic broken statue that the speaker can never "put together entirely, / Pieced, glued, and properly jointed" (1–2). As the poem progresses, the Colossus changes from a statue to a wilderness of "weedy acres" (13) and a "hill of black cypress" (19). Then it reverts to a statue with an ear (25). Like a priestess, the speaker tends to the idol, laboring "to dredge the silt from [its] throat" (9) and trying "to mend the immense skull-plates and clear / The bald white tumuli of [its] eyes" (14–15). At the same time, she is intimate with the statue, crawling over it (12), eating her lunch there (19), and squatting in its ear (24–25). At the end of the poem, the speaker focuses on herself, stating that, as she sits in its ear, she is comfortably sheltered from the wind. At the same time, she has lost her curiosity and her joy of life because she no longer listens for the sound of a new ship to arrive.

Because the speaker addresses the statue as "father" (17), a number of critics regard this poem as a description of Plath's relationship with her father. But Margaret Dickie Uroff says that "nothing in this poem demands that single interpretation" and suggests instead that "the colossus is not the actual father but the creative father . . . Plath's private god of poetry" (90). Looked at in this way, the poem takes on universal qualities by describing creative paralysis. The Colossus, a symbol of creativity, is broken, and no matter how hard the speaker tries to mend it, it remains shattered. She cannot be creative because she is unable to clear the silt from the statue's mouth and thus it cannot speak to give her inspiration. Incapacitated, the speaker, "married to a shadow" (28), is unable to be creative and becomes shadowlike herself. Steven Gould Axelrod explains that "existence in and as a shadow in 'The Colossus' thus represents the creative half-life that is, rather than the full life that might have been" (295).

Technically, the speaker uses a conversational tone. Written in free verse, there is no rhyme and no regular pattern, except for the six five-line stanzas. Rhythmically, Plath writes in iambic meter, a form she often uses in her later poetry because, according to Eileen M. Aird, she felt its "elasticity . . . was much closer to the rhythms of spoken English" than styles she had used earlier (3).

"Daddy" (*Ariel*), 1962

In Plath's angry poem, Daddy is a "father—whether purely an artistic construct or a derivative of the poet's father—[who] is a fabrication of a persona who attempts to exorcise her childish view of her daddy" (Nance and Jones, 124). Plath herself described it as a "poem spoken by a girl with an Electra complex. Her father died while she thought he was God. Her case is complicated by the fact that her father was also a Nazi and her mother very possibly part Jewish. In the daughter the two strains marry and paralyse [sic] each other—she has to act out the awful little allegory once over before she is free of it" (quoted in Ted Hughes, "Notes on Poems," 293; note 183). In "Daddy," the female speaker expresses her feelings of oppression and hatred caused by an image she had created of her father as deity and devil. Plath, however, moves beyond this portrait of one individual's personal despair into a broader picture of oppression and victimization. As critic George Steiner argues, "Daddy" is a poem that "achieves the classic art of generalization, translating a private, obviously intolerable hurt into a code of plain statement, of instantaneously public images which concern us all" (quoted in Wagner, *Critical Essays*, 1–2).

In the first twelve stanzas, the daughter, who loves and hates her father, describes "a childhood version of the father which persists into adulthood" (Nance and Jones, 125). She detests him for confining her, viewing him as a "black shoe" (2) in which she has lived claustrophobically, "Barely daring to breathe or Achoo" (5), for thirty years. A "Marble-heavy" (8), "Ghastly statue" (9), he has overpowered her. Because her infantile version of her father "dwarfs and restricts her own life . . . she must ritually destroy the memory of her father" (Aird, 80), and so she tells him, "Daddy, I have had to kill you" (6). Although the adult daughter hates him, as a child she loved him, "pray[ing] to recover" him (14) and seeking to find him through his German heritage by learning his language and by searching for him in various European towns. Unable to locate him, the daughter, in the next stanzas, reveals how she tried to join him by trying to commit suicide to "get back, back, back to you" (59). Saved from this attempt, she "made a model" (64) of her father and married him. Far from finding satisfaction, she becomes even more oppressed because her husband loved "the rack and the screw" (66), which are historical instruments of torture. Now she faces two people she needs to destroy—her childish vision of her father and the husband made in his image. Using magic, she finally gets rid of the mental images she has of her father by driving "a stake in [his] fat black heart" (76).

Her final words, "I'm through" (80), "imply both that the magic has worked its power of dispossession and also that the speaker is left with nothing. Dispossessed in the *imago* which has defined her own identity and with which she has been obsessed, she is psychically finished, depleted" (Nance and Jones, 127–128).

This psychological analysis is only one aspect of the poem; Plath moves her poem out of the personal space and into the "stifling political world" (Narbeshuber, 190) where her speaker engages in universal struggles. One way she does this is by including references to the world: "Atlantic" (11), "Polish town" (16), "wars" (18), "Dachau, Auschwitz, Belsen" (33), "snows of the Tyrol," the Alpine region in Austria and northern Italy, and "Vienna" (36). She also looks at world events, making her father into a German Nazi and herself into a suffering Jew, thus using actual historical images of the torturer and the tortured. Seeing herself as a victim of the Nazis, the speaker embraces all oppressed peoples and reacts against the oppressors, but even as she attempts to overpower the oppressive Nazi father whom she still loves and desires, she shows that "the exploitation of women in a patriarchal society is in part due to women's compliance in the sado-masochism involved" (Markley, 16) because, as Plath writes, "Every woman adores a Fascist, / The boot in the face" (48–49). But the speaker, in spite of her fascination with domination, continues to fight against and finally destroys her oppressors. She concludes by showing that she is not alone in condemning those who control others; the villagers, who "never liked" him (77), celebrate Daddy's destruction by "dancing and stamping" on him (78).

Plath develops her theme of victim/victimizer by using rich imagery. Her first metaphor is the boot, which she turns into various meanings. Uroff paints a vivid picture of Plath's use of this image: the daughter "starts out imagining herself as a prisoner living like a foot in the black shoe of her father. Then she casts her father in her own role; he becomes 'one grey [sic] toe / Big as a Frisco seal,' and then quickly she is looking for his foot, his root. Next, she reverts to the original boot identity, and she is the one with 'The boot in the face.' Immediately she finds 'A cleft in your chin instead of your foot.' At the end, she sees the villagers stamping on him" (159–160). Uroff concludes by noting that "she moves from booted to booter as her father reverses the direction" (160).

"Daddy" is full of Nazi and Jewish imagery: "German tongue" (16); "Barb wire snare" (26); "Dachau, Auschwitz, Belsen," sites of World War II German death camps (33); "Luftwaffe," the German air force of World War II (42); "neat mustache," a reminder of Hitler (43); "Aryan eye, bright blue," a reference to the Nazis' idea that the blond, blue-eyed Aryan race was superior to others (44); "Panzer," German for armored tank (45); "swastika" (46); "Fascist" (48); and "Meinkampf" (65), the title of Adolf Hitler's autobiography and political manifesto which in translation means "My Struggle." These allusions depict the father as an evil, domineering, unfeeling man, a "brute" (49, 50). They also show the victim and the tormentors as part of worldwide problems and situations.

Plath incorporates two additional images, the devil and a vampire, to show the evils of domination, in particular, the harm caused by a patriarchal society that marginalizes women. The daughter declares that her father is "no less a devil" (54) even though he has a cleft chin instead of cleft hooves, a characteristic of the devil. And, in the last two stanzas, she views her husband, a model of her father, as a vampire who has drunk her blood during their seven years of marriage. She destroys her father by driving a stake through his heart, the traditional method of killing vampires.

All of these images of tormentors develop Plath's theme of victimization as the speaker confronts her own suffering and speaks out against this terrible situation.

Although the thirty-year-old speaker selects serious images to depict her cruel father, she uses childlike techniques to portray herself, making her seem more vulnerable. By beginning with a story of living in a shoe, she evokes the image of the nursery rhyme old woman who lived in a shoe. Throughout the poem, she uses simple language, selecting many short, one-syllable words and lacing her diction with childish terms such as "Daddy" (6, 75, 80), "Achoo" (5), "gobbledy-goo" (43), and "pretty red heart" (56). She fills the stanzas with the repetitive rhythms and rhymes of children's poetry, in particular using words rhyming with "do," "shoe," "you," and "Jew." These short rhyming words not only add to the vision of the speaker as a vulnerable child but also produce a staccato effect, helping convey her fury.

Although a number of critics see this poem as a purely biographical portrayal of Plath's father and husband, the poem is much more than this. Jones describes it in this way: "The poem is a terrifyingly intimate portrait, but it achieves something much more than the expression of a personal and despairing grief. . . . The tortured mind of the heroine reflects the tortured mind of our age" (236).

"Lady Lazarus" (*Ariel*), 1962

"Lady Lazarus" is another of Plath's most highly regarded writings. Plath said, "The speaker is a woman who has the great and terrible gift of being reborn. The only trouble is, she has to die first. She is the Phoenix, the libertarian spirit, what you will. She is also just a good, plain, very resourceful woman" (quoted in Ted Hughes, "Notes on Poems," 294; note 198). "Lady Lazarus"

THIS PAINTING BY LEON BONNAT DEPICTS THE BIBLICAL STORY FROM THE GOSPEL OF JOHN IN WHICH JESUS RESURRECTS LAZARUS FROM THE DEAD.

shows the struggle between a female who wants to be independent and others who seek to control her as she recovers from a suicide attempt.

The primary image Plath draws on is the biblical Lazarus, for whom her character is named. In the Bible, there are two separate men called Lazarus, and Plath uses both in her poem. The first, found in the Gospel of John, is Jesus's friend from Bethany, the brother of Mary and Martha, who died and whose body begins decomposing before Jesus comes to his home and raises him from the dead. Lazarus emerges from the grave with his hands and feet bound with strips of cloth and his face wrapped in a cloth or napkin (John 11:44). Plath's "Lady Lazarus" uses a number of images that point to this biblical figure: "miracle" (4, 55), "peel off the napkin" (10), "grave" (17), "cave" (17), "unwrap me hand and foot" (28), and "rocked shut" (39). Like Jesus's friend, Lady Lazarus has been miraculously resurrected from the dead and is having the cloths of death removed from her body.

The second biblical Lazarus, found in the Gospel of Luke, is a beggar "covered with sores" that "dogs would come and lick" (Luke 16:20–21). In this story, a rich man refuses to help Lazarus, who dies and goes to heaven. When the rich man also dies, he is tormented in the fires of hell. Seeing Lazarus sitting by Abraham, the rich man calls on Lazarus to bring him cool water, but Abraham stops him, telling the rich man: "remember that during your lifetime you received your good things, and Lazarus in like manner evil things; but now he is comforted here, and you are in agony" (Luke 16:25). Lady Lazarus, like the beggar, is "skin and bones" (33), covered with "worms" (42), and filled with "scars" (58) and sores. Although Lady Lazarus now lives in anguish, as Lazarus did on earth, her victimizers will be in torment later because she, like the beggar who is well-fed after death, will rise up and "eat men like air" (84) and achieve the final victory. By using references to this second Lazarus, Plath makes her poem into "both a plea for help and a damning indictment of the unwilling helper" (Hall, 109).

To establish Lady Lazarus's relationship with her various enemies, Plath uses four sets of images to show how others view her. In the first stanzas, Lady Lazarus talks to her unnamed "enemy" (11) who sees her as some type of nonhuman material—a "lampshade" (5), a "paperweight" (7), and "fine / Jew linen" (9). Throughout the middle of the poem, as she addresses the "Gentlemen, ladies" (30) who stare with lascivious interest at her because she has been saved from suicide, she shows that they see her as merely a physical body: "nose" (13), "eye pits" (13), "teeth" (13), "hands" (31), "knees" (32), "skin and bone" (33), and "hair" (66). Then, when she turns to the Nazi "Herr Doktor," "Herr Enemy" (65, 66), she illustrates that he regards her for her monetary value, for she is an "opus" (67), a "valuable" (68), "pure gold" (69), "ash" (73) which is used to make a "cake of soap" (76), a "wedding ring" (77), and a "gold filling" (78). Finally, as she achieves rebirth and addresses "Herr God, Herr Lucifer" (79), she becomes a spiritual being with "red hair" (83) who "eat[s] men" (84).

By using these different images, Plath shows that none of the outsiders sees Lady Lazarus as an independent, whole person. To them, she is a fragmented being. As Rosenblatt explains, she becomes "a different person for each of her audiences, and yet none of her identities is bearable for her" (39). He goes on to list the different identities: "For the Nazi Doktor, she is a Jew, whose body must be burned; for the 'peanut-crunching crowd,' she is a stripteaser; for the medical audience, she is a wonder, whose scars and heartbeat are astonishing; for the religious audience, she is a miraculous figure, whose hair and clothes are as valuable as a saint's relics. And when she turns to her audience in the middle of the poem to describe her career in suicide, she becomes a self-conscious performer" (39). After her body is burned to ash by Herr Doktor, Lady Lazarus plays the role of the mythical Phoenix who is resurrected from the ashes. As a spirit, she is now able to fight against those who have imprisoned her—men, gods, doctor, and Nazis. Lady Lazarus, then, like Lazarus of Bethany, is resurrected, and, like Lazarus the beggar, triumphs over her enemies.

Written as a dramatic monologue, "Lady Lazarus" brings to mind one other Lazarus, the one mentioned in T. S. Eliot's dramatic monologue, "The Love Song of J. Alfred Prufrock." Eliot's timid speaker, who wishes he had the courage to tell the truths of life, wonders if he dares to declare, "I am Lazarus, come from the dead, / Come back to tell you all, I shall tell you all" (94–95). Unlike hesitant Prufrock who ends up saying nothing, Plath's protagonist lashes out against those who have trapped her into roles she does not wish to play and "tells all."

Plath has been highly praised for the poetic techniques she uses in "Lady Lazarus," a poem Eileen M. Aird calls "a supreme example of Sylvia Plath's skill as an artist" (83). Plath forms a "highly wrought poem" with "polar opposition between the terrible gaiety of its form and the fiercely uncompromising seriousness of its subject" (Aird, 83–84). One of Plath's main techniques is the use of colloquial language. She engages in a conversational style ("I have done it again" [1]); adds American slang ("trash" [23], "shoves" [27], "the big strip tease" [29], "feels like hell" [46], "knocks me out" [56]); includes pat sayings ("Dying / Is an art, like everything else" [43–44]); uses an obvious, singsong internal rhyme ("grave cave" [17], "turn and burn" [71]); and incorporates repetition ("Ash, ash" [73], "Beware / Beware" [80–81]). The three-line terza rima stanzas are composed of off-rhymes or slant rhymes, which generally cross over to include two stanzas, such as in stanzas one and two, where she uses "again" / "then" / "skin" (1, 2, 4); and in stanzas three and four, where she rhymes "fine" / "linen" / "napkin" (8, 9, 10). This pattern continues throughout the poem.

The imagery in this poem is striking. Not only does she use the Lazarus stories, Plath also includes historical images of great suffering. Although some critics have criticized her for taking images of Nazism, Jewishness, and the Holocaust to describe her personal anguish, others support their use, arguing that "these allusions to historical events form part of the speaker's fragmented identity and allow Plath to portray a kind of eternal victim. . . . the holocaust serves her as a metaphor for the death-and-life battle between the self and a deadly enemy" (Rosenblatt, 42–43).

Many critics, looking at the poem narrowly as a type of biography of Plath's life, regard Lady Lazarus's deadly enemy as Plath's father and/or husband, and they interpret the poem as a feminist struggle between men and a victorious woman. To them, Plath is an unstoppable Lady Lazarus who rises up in a "triumph of vitality" (Broe, 175) to destroy men and escape "from a life of abuse and nightmare to one of liberation" (Markey, 122). She is a "searingly self-confident" woman (Van Dyne, 55) who finds her "true identity as a triumphant resurrecting goddess, the fully liberated, fiery true self" (Kroll, 118–119). Possessing "independent creative powers," she is "a phoenix, a flame of released bodily energy" (Bundtzen, 33–34). These interpretations all limit "Lady Lazarus" to being a confessional poem of Plath's life. If it were only this, it would be an interesting work, but not a lasting piece of art. But "Lady Lazarus" has been popular for decades because it encompasses a much broader theme—the victimization and triumph of any marginalized, abused person. Lisa Narbeshuber states that Plath "moves out of the skin of the *individual* and sketches out the social game, the *intersubjective* complexes rather than the *inner strife*" that many critics focus on (187). Narbeshuber goes on to explain that "more than an attack on the male (or in particular her husband or father), her poetry confronts the mentality of the status quo" (187) that limits people by forcing them into narrow roles.

Thus, "Lady Lazarus" is a highly regarded poem for two reasons: theme and technique. Aird sums up the critical position well, stating that although it is a poem of intense personal suffering, it "is also a poem of social criticism with a strong didactic intent, and a work of art which reveals great technical and intellectual ability" (84).

"Metaphors" (*The Colossus*), 1959

A playful poem, "Metaphors" is a riddle told by a pregnant woman who happily makes up images. After initially identifying herself as "a riddle" (1), the speaker uses a variety of metaphors to show that she is big, calling herself "an elephant" (2), "a ponderous house" (2), "a melon strolling on two tendrils" (3), and "a cow in calf" (7). She also suggests that something new is about to appear by referring to herself as "a means" (7) and "a stage" (7). Other metaphors in the poem relate to the speaker's condition. The "loaf" (5) is a common euphemism for pregnancy, while the "fat purse" (6) is her expanding stomach, bloated as if she had "eaten a bag of green apples" (8). The unborn child is called "red fruit" (4), "yeasty rising" (5), and "new-minted" money (6); its skin is "ivory" (4), and its developing bones are "fine timbers" (4). The "train" (9) is pregnancy, and the "nine syllables" (1) are the nine months of pregnancy. Lightheartedly, Plath uses all of these images as metaphors for pregnancy, a condition lasting nine months that causes a woman's midsection to swell up like a growing fruit and be supported by two tendril-like legs. The developing fetus, growing bigger and bigger like rising bread, is a new, valuable creation, similar to newly minted money. The pregnant woman cannot stop her pregnancy any more than a person aboard a moving train can get off it.

The form of the poem follows the meaning. Like a nine-month pregnancy, it is made up of nine lines of nine syllables each.

Literary Reception

As Mary Kinzie points out, there are "two 'periods' of Plath criticism; the first is divided from the second by her death on February 11, 1963. Until that time, the reviews of *The Colossus* . . . had been brief, reserved, entirely conventional" (283). Some of the early reviews, written in 1960 and 1961 when *The Colossus* first appeared, mention that Plath "simply writes good poetry" in "an individual manner," but is too tricky with "wordage" (quoted in Kinzie, 284–285). Others feel that even though her "outlook is gloomy, . . . she is exhilarating to read" (quoted in Kinzie, 284). At least one critic commended Plath's poetic techniques, calling her "impressive for control of form and tone, appropriateness of rhythmic variation within the poem, and vocabulary and observation which are often surprising, and always accurate" (Myers, 31).

With the publication of *Ariel* in 1965, she achieved iconic status, but, as Katha Pollitt writes, it was "the wrong kind of fame, for it was based on the notion that her poems could be read as if they were a suicide note that 'explained' her death" (68). Plath's poetry was regarded as "confessional," a term used by M. L. Rosenthal in 1967 to describe "highly charged" poetry narrated by a speaker who is "at the centre of the poem in such a way as to make his [or her] psychological vulnerability and shame an embodiment of . . . civilization" (69). Whether critics admired or condemned *Ariel*, most looked upon the poems as Plath's personal confessions about herself and, as a result, analyzed them as either biography or psychological case studies. One analyst criticized *Ariel* for asking "us to feel emotions based on a delirium we do not share," and concluded that "it is best viewed as a case study" (quoted in Kinzie, 299), a point often reiterated because many felt that there is a difficulty "of separating her work from her psychology" since "disorder, suffering, even madness are not, in themselves, necessarily interesting" (quoted in Kinzie, 302). But others praised Plath's "confessional" poems, pronouncing that "the personal tragedy somehow reinforces poetry" (quoted in Kinzie, 302). There were a few critics who thought that viewing the poems as confessional was "unnecessary to the experience of these poems [and] rendered them less rather than more accessible" (Drake, 43), and at least one reviewer recognized *Ariel* as "one of the most powerful books since the war" (Porter, 46).

Beginning with the publication of *Ariel*, Plath's works have been enthusiastically received. For instance, *Crossing the Water* was acclaimed as a book "of perfectly realised [sic] works" written by "a front-rank artist in the process of discovering her true power" (Porter, 46). Another commended it as "a substantial eyeful from an unflagging sharp sensibility; a small pageant in insistent vernacular; a book of vivid austerities" (West, 50). *Winter Trees* was similarly well-received, the poems praised for their "complicated use of colours" (Grant, 53) that were written with "the familiar Plath daring, the same feel of bits of frightened, vibrant, indignant consciousness translated instantly into words and images that blend close, experienced horror and icy, sardonic control" (Brownstone, 55). In 1981, *The Collected Poems* received special acclamation. Hailed as the "most important book of poetry published this year," it "makes clear that [Plath] was one of the most remarkable poets of her time" (Lerner, 64, 65). Another extolled it as a "beautiful book" written by a "superb craftsman" who is "dazzlingly inventive" (Pollitt, 68, 69). Plath's poems were considered "such virtuoso performances in technique, such spellbinding expressions of emotion" (Wagner-Martin, *Sylvia Plath*, 11) that the Pulitzer Prize for Poetry was awarded to her *Collected Poems* in 1982.

Knowing that Plath had arranged the order of her *Ariel* poems differently than they had appeared in 1965, people looked forward to the publication of *Ariel: The*

Restored Edition. When it appeared in 2004, they were not disappointed. Although the poems were not new, the book had a different tone. Instead of concluding with an attitude of absolute despair, as the 1965 volume had with "Wintering," this restored version ended on a note of triumph, with "spring" being the final word.

In spite of the popular appeal of Plath's poetry, a number of critics dismiss her as a major American poet because they have continued to regard her as a confessional poet, a term that, by the late 1970s, had become a derogatory way to criticize the self-indulgence of writers who wrote only of themselves. Thus, critics such as Helen Vendler, commenting in 1982, see Plath's works as narrow because of her "refusal to generalize . . . beyond her own case," which stopped her from writing "about the human condition" and from "seeing herself as one of many" (5). Even recent critics continue to look at Plath's poetry as nothing more than comments about her personal life. For example, Elisabeth Bronfen, writing in 1998, thinks that Plath's "life and her poetry are so inextricably implicated that we can do nothing but read her poetry within the biographical appraisal that has reworked her life for us" (7).

However, others argue that her works are universal cries of suffering. In particular, feminists have embraced her poetry, asserting that Plath writes about universal experiences of women as she details the victimization and entrapment of women, rages against men who have oppressive power, and declares her independence. Males also find Plath's poems relevant to them because they describe emotions experienced by all human beings.

Plath's poems certainly seem to have a widespread appeal. They have not lost their popularity in the more than four decades since they first appeared. Not only do her volumes of poetry continue to sell well, but her individual poems, particularly "Ariel," "Lady Lazarus," and "Daddy," appear in countless anthologies of American literature and of poetry. She has come to be highly regarded for her bitter humor, superb craftsmanship, feminist views, expressions of intense anguish, and ability to speak for the suffering and downtrodden. Pollitt speaks for many fans when she says, "there was no other voice like hers on earth" (69).

Gwyneth Paltrow portrayed Sylvia Plath in the 2003 film *Sylvia*.

Chapter 5

Plath's Place in Literature

SYLVIA PLATH was not a well-known writer during her life-time. Even though she had published two books, *The Colossus* and *The Bell Jar*, they were neither widely read nor extensively reviewed. But with her suicide on February 11, 1963, Plath gained instant fame as a symbol of a troubled poet victimized by a hostile society. From the month of her death to the present, her poetry, fiction, non-fiction, and drama have been regularly printed in periodicals and books, and they have been eagerly purchased by a "quasi-cultish audience—the sort that rarely forms around an author, living or dead—[which] bought almost anything written by her" (Alexander, *Rough Magic*, 334).

When Ted Hughes, as Plath's heir and executor, published *Ariel* in 1965, "it was a sensation, with a double-page spread in *Time* magazine setting off a frenzy. Women were joining consciousness-raising groups, and Plath was often the center of the discussion" (McCullough, xii). Biographer Paul Alexander reports that according to *Time* and *Newsweek*, "in its first year of publication in England alone, the book sold more than fifteen thousand copies—probably a conservative estimate. Sales in America easily surpassed those in England." Alexander notes that it continued to sell more than half a million copies in its first twenty years, "making it one of the best-selling volumes of poetry to be published in England or America in the twentieth century" (*Rough Magic*, 343–344).

By the time *The Bell Jar* was published in America in 1971, Plath was an established cult figure. With her name well-known, the novel immediately became a runaway success, listed on the *New York Times* best-seller list for twenty-four weeks, "an unprecedented accomplishment for a first novel written by an author known primarily for her poetry." When a paperback copy came out a year later, all 375,000 copies of the first printing, plus a second and third printing, sold out in one month (Alexander, *Rough Magic*, 348). The book has continued to sell well.

In 1971, in addition to *The Bell Jar*, two highly praised, popular volumes of poetry were published: *Crossing the Water* and *Winter Trees* (which was published in a U.S. edition in 1972). Plath acquired an even larger following with the 1971 publication of A. Alvarez's book on suicide, *The Savage God*, in which he used Plath as a prime example. In 1973, Marjorie Perloff wrote, "Sylvia Plath has become a true cult figure. At this writing, the Savile Book Shop in Georgetown, Washington, D. C., has a huge window display in which copies of *The Colossus*, *The Bell Jar*, *Ariel*, and *Crossing the Water* encircle a large photograph of Sylvia Plath, which rests against a copy of A. Alvarez's *The Savage God: A Study of Suicide*, that ultimate tribute to Sylvia Plath as our Extremist Poet par excellence" (quoted in Alexander, *Rough Magic*, 352).

In spite of Plath's popularity, *Letters Home* (1975) and *Johnny Panic and the Bible of Dreams* (1977), a book of early Plath writings, sold poorly. However, the long-awaited complete edition of Plath's poetry met with instant success when it appeared in 1981. For *The Collected Poems*, Sylvia Plath won the Pulitzer Prize for Poetry in 1982, an unusual occurrence since the Pulitzer is almost always awarded to living poets (Wagner-Martin, *Sylvia Plath*, 11).

Three other major writings by Sylvia Plath have been published since: *The Collected Poems: The Journals of Sylvia Plath* (1982), *The Unabridged Journals of Sylvia Plath, 1950–1962* (2000), and *Ariel: The Restored*

Edition (2004). All have been of great interest to critics, biographers, readers, and fans.

Plath's suicide caused such notoriety that, for decades, her life seemed to overshadow her works. Immediately idolized as a "madwoman" poet, she was seen as an angry and defiant artist driven to her untimely death. Unfortunately, the "confessional" label meant, for a time, that many perceived her writings as comments about her life instead of pieces of art. As Christina Britzolakis points out in her introduction to *Sylvia Plath and the Theatre of Mourning*, Plath "became something other than a writer—an oracular priestess, a hysterical patient, a sacrificial victim—and the materiality of her writing was brushed aside as merely epiphenomenal" (3).

Feminist critics fell into the same "trap of diagnosis: of turning Plath, as the confessional thesis had done, into a martyr and victim (this time, however, of a culture in which genius was defined as a male preserve) or of turning her writing into a narrative of self-discovery or psychic rebirth which redeems the social and psychic divisions she could not overcome in life" (Britzolakis, 4). Many women sympathized with *The Bell Jar*'s heroine, who is disgusted by the sexist 1950s society in which she lives. They also identified with Sylvia Plath, who, according to their view, was destroyed by the patriarchal society. Her followers hated Hughes, looking at him as a monster responsible for his wife's death. It is assumed that radical feminists are the ones who repeatedly traveled to Plath's grave in England, where they chiseled away the name "Hughes" on her tombstone, which reads "Sylvia Plath Hughes" (Alexander, *Rough Magic*, 363). Although many people look upon Plath as a feminist, her friend Jillian Becker emphatically states that Plath "herself was no feminist; not, anyway, if feminism means scorning the traditional woman's role of wife and mother, homemaker and housekeeper" (71). Even though she "raged against her dead father and the faithless husband—the one for having died and been German, the other for being faithless and as brutal as a Nazi—she did not hate men in general. Far from it" (Becker, 71–72).

Today, although many people still look upon her as a confessional writer or a feminist icon, her writings are also studied and praised as works of art separate from her life.

She has remained a major literary figure in the years since her death. *The Bell Jar* and many of her poems are required reading in high school.

Scholars remain fascinated by her work and life. Major biographies have appeared continuously since 1977. The most recent ones are those by Christina Britzolakis (2001) and Diane Middlebrook (2003). In addition, a number of essay collections have appeared; probably of greatest importance are those edited by Charles Newman (1979), Edward Butscher (1979), Linda W. Wagner (1984), and Paul Alexander (1985). Even today new collections, including one edited by Jo Gill (2006) and another by Anita Helle (2007), are printed.

Plath's status as a major writer is also seen in the way other writers regard her. She has been the subject of poems written by Anne Sexton ("Sylvia's Death" and "Wanting to Die") and feminist Erica Jong ("In Sylvia Plath Country"). An entire book of poems written about Plath appeared in 1996. Entitled *About Sylvia/Poems by Diane Ackerman*, it contains poems by such distinguished authors as Diane Ackerman, John Berryman, Rachel Hadas, Robert Lowell, Anne Sexton, and Richard Wilbur. Probably the best well-known book of poems about Plath was written by her husband, Ted Hughes. *Birthday Letters*, a series of poems about Hughes's relationship with Sylvia Plath, appeared in 1998.

LETTERS HOME, A COMPILATION OF 696 LETTERS SAVED BY PLATH'S MOTHER, AURELIA, WAS MADE INTO A BOOK AND, LATER, PERFORMED ON STAGE.

In popular culture, Plath has become, as Kate A. Baldwin writes, "a cottage industry (21)," featured in music, films, and drama. Beginning in the mid–1970s and continuing into the present, musicians have set her poetry to vocal and instrumental music, "Lady Lazarus" and "Ariel" being the most popular choices. Probably the best-known song about Plath is "I Wish I had a Sylvia Plath," released in 2001 by rock star Ryan Adams. Major Plath films include Larry Peerce's *The Bell Jar* (1979) and Christine Jeffs's 2003 motion picture *Sylvia*, starring Gwyneth Paltrow. The author and her works have been mentioned in popular media, including the 1999 movie *Ten Things I Hate About You,* in which the female lead reads *The Bell Jar*, and an installment of *The Gilmore Girls* in which Rory, the main character, reads Plath's diaries. Plath's works have also been turned into dramas, such as *Letters Home*, a play by Rose Leiman Goldemberg that was staged in 1979, and a 2003 off-Broadway production based on *The Bell Jar*.

In the decades since her death, Sylvia Plath has become famous, not only for her sad life, but also as both a poet and a novelist. Harper editor Frances McCullough states that Plath has become "the last of the major poets read widely . . . [and] a feminist heroine whose single pub-lished novel had spoken directly to the hearts of more than one generation" (xi). "[C]hampioned, deified, criti-cized, and gossiped about" (Wagner-Martin, *Sylvia Plath,* 247), Sylvia Plath has won a permanent place in literature, recognized as one of the greatest writers of the twentieth century whose writings inspire readers with their power, artistry, and independent voice.

Works

Prose
The Bell Jar (1963)
Johnny Panic and the Bible of Dreams: Short Stories, Prose, and Diary Excerpts (1977)

Poetry
The Colossus and Other Poems (1960)
Ariel (1965)
Crossing the Water (1971)
Winter Trees (1971)
The Collected Poems, edited by Ted Hughes (1981)
Ariel: The Restored Edition (2004)

Journals and Letters
Letters Home: Correspondence, 1950–1963 (1975)
The Journals of Sylvia Plath (1982)
The Unabridged Journals of Sylvia Plath, 1950–1962 (2000)

Other Writings
American Poetry Now: A Selection of the Best Poems by Modern American Writers, edited by Sylvia Plath (1961)
The Bed Book (1976)
The It-Doesn't-Matter Suit (1996)
Three Women: A Monologue for Three Voices (1968)
The Magic Mirror: A Study of the Double in Two of Dostoevsky's Novels (1989)

Filmography

Films

2003　*Sylvia*. Motion Picture. Directed by Christine Jeffs. Starring Gwyneth Paltrow and Daniel Craig. Universal Studios. BBC.

1999　*The Master Poets Collection: Sylvia Plath: Growth of a Poet*. PBS Movie. Monterey Video.

1999　*Voices and Visions: Sylvia Plath*. Video. Interviews with Sylvia Plath's mother, and Sylvia's reading of her poetry. Winstar Home Entertainment.

1991　*Lady Lazarus: The Work of Sylvia Plath*. Film by Sandra Lahrire. England.

1979　*The Bell Jar*. Directed by Larry Peerce. Screenplay by Majorie Kellogg. Starring Marilyn Hassett, Julie Harris, and Anne Jackson. Avco-Embassy.

Audio Tapes

2000　*Sylvia Plath Reads*. By Sylvia Plath. Harper Audio.

1999　*Sylvia Plath*. By Sylvia Plath. Random House Audio Books.

1999　*The Bell Jar*. Read by Frances McDormand. Harper Audio.

1999　*The Bell Jar*. Read by Fiona Shaw. Penguin Audio Books.

1997　*The It-Doesn't-Matter Suit*. Sylvia Plath's children's story. Read by Andrew Sachs. Penguin Audio Books.

Chronology

1932
October 27: Born in Boston to Aurelia Schober and Otto Emil Plath.

1935
Brother Warren is born.

1936
Plath family moves to Winthrop, Massachusetts.

1940
Father dies of complications following leg amputation due to diabetes.

1942
Plath and Schober families move to Wellesley, Massachusetts; Aurelia teaches at Boston University.

1942–1950
Tries to publish poems and stories while at school at Wellesley.

1950–1953
Attends Smith College on scholarships.

1953
Summer: In New York City as guest editor for *Mademoiselle*. Receives outpatient electroconvulsive shock therapy for depression; attempts suicide, is hospitalized, and recovers.

1954
Returns to Smith College for spring semester; attends summer school at Harvard on a scholarship.

1955
Graduates from Smith College summa cum laude; receives Fulbright fellowship and attends Newnham College at Cambridge University in England.

1956
June 16: Marries poet Ted Hughes.

1957
Receives degree from Cambridge; moves to Massachusetts with husband; teaches freshman English at Smith College.

1958
Moves to Boston with husband; works part-time jobs; attends Boston University to study poetry with Robert Lowell; resumes therapy.

1959
Summer: Tours United States by car.
Fall: Lives at writers' Yaddo Colony in New York.
December: Moves to London with her husband.

1960
April 1: First child, Frieda Rebecca Hughes, is born.
October: *The Colossus and Other Poems* is published in Great Britain.

1961
February: Miscarries; has an appendectomy.
September: Hughes family moves to Devon, England.

1962
January 17: Son, Nicholas Farrar Hughes, is born.
May: *The Colossus and Other Poems* is published in the United States.
September: Separates from her husband.
Fall: Writes many poems that will be published in *Ariel*.
December: Moves to the Yeats house in London with children.

1963
January: *The Bell Jar* is published under the pseudonym Victoria Lucas.
February 11: Commits suicide.

1965
Ted publishes *Ariel* in Great Britain.

1966
Ariel is published in the United States.
The Bell Jar is published in Great Britain under the name Sylvia Plath.

1971
The Bell Jar and *Crossing the Water* are published in the United States; *Crossing the Water* and *Winter Trees* are published in Great Britain.

1972
Winter Trees is published in the United States.

1975
Letters Home is published in the United States.

1976
Letters Home is published in Great Britain.

1977
Johnny Panic and the Bible of Dreams is published in Great Britain.

1979
Johnny Panic and the Bible of Dreams is published in the United States.

1981
The Collected Poems is published in the United States and Great Britain.

1982
The Collected Poems wins Pulitzer Prize in poetry; *The Journals of Sylvia Plath* is published in the United States.

2000
The Unabridged Journals of Sylvia Plath, 1950–1962 is published.

2004
Ariel: The Restored Edition is published.

Notes

Chapter 1

p. 12, par. 2, Paul Alexander's biography is especially useful in providing information about the Plath family. Aurelia Plath visited with him for "countless hours" (xiii), providing him with facts about the life of her daughter and her family. *See Rough Magic: A Biography of Sylvia Plath* (New York: Viking Penguin, 1991. Reprinted. Cambridge, MA: Da Capo Press, 1999).

p. 12, par. 3, For more information on the writing of Otto Plath's book, *see* Alexander, *Rough Magic*, 21–22.

p. 20, par. 1, For a close view of Sylvia Plath as a college student, *see* Nancy Hunter Steiner, *A Closer Look at Ariel: A Memory of Sylvia Plath* (New York: Popular Library, 1973), 1–69.

p. 22, par. 1, Catherine Thompson writes an excellent analysis of Plath's affliction with this hormonal disorder. *See* "'Dawn Poems in Blood': Sylvia Plath and PMS," *Tri-Quarterly* 80 (Winter 1990–1991), 221–249.

p. 26, par. 2, For information on Plath's type of mental illness, *see* Frederick K. Goodwin and Kay Redfield Jamison, "Manic-Depressive Illness and Creativity" in *Manic-Depressive Illness* (New York: Oxford University Press, 1990), 342–356; and Gordon Claridge, "Creativity and Madness: Clues from Modern Psychiatric Diagnosis" in *Genius and the Mind: Studies of Creativity and*

Temperament, ed. Andrew Steptoe (New York: Oxford University Press, 1998), 237–238.

p. 29, par. 1, For more information on the summer of 1954 which Plath spent at Harvard, *see* Steiner, 69–110.

p. 34, par. 1, Aurelia Plath described her relationship with her daughter. *See* Alexander, *Rough Magic*, 220–225.

p. 43, par. 3, For further information about the breakup of Ted and Sylvia's marriage, *see* Alexander, *Rough Magic*, 275–318; Linda W. Wagner-Martin, *Sylvia Plath: A Biography* (New York: St. Martin's Press, 1987), 204–233; and Edward Butscher, *Sylvia Plath: Method and Madness* (New York: Seabury Press, 1976), 296–337.

p. 45, par. 1, A vivid account of Sylvia Plath's last days and funeral are found in Jillian Becker, *Giving Up: The Last Days of Sylvia Plath* (New York: St. Martin's Press, 2002).

p. 50, par. 2, For Aurelia Plath's views on the reason for her daughter's suicide, *see* Diane Middlebrook, "Notes to Pages 209–212" in *Her Husband: Hughes and Plath—A Marriage* (New York: Viking, 2003), 331.

Chapter 2

p. 53, par. 1, For further information on the 1930s, *see* Foster Rhea Dulles, *Twentieth Century America* (Boston: Houghton Mifflin, 1945), 357–463; Dwight Lowell Dumond, *America in Our Time: 1896–1946* (New York: Henry Holt and Company, 1947), 469–589; Frank Freidel, *America in the Twentieth Century* (New York: Alfred A. Knopf, 1960), 276–360; and Daniel Snowman, *America Since 1920* (New York: Harper and Row, 1968), 42–70.

p. 54, par. 1, For further information on the war years, *see* Daniel F. Davis and Norman Lunger, *A History of the United States Since 1945* (New York: Scholastic, 1987), 18; Dulles, 467–567; Dumond, 590–675; Freidel, 361–460; and Snowman, 103–116.

p. 55, par. 3, Many people felt that the Rosenbergs, particularly Ethel, were unfairly punished. Looking at the situation decades later, Ellen Schrecker agrees with this analysis. Writing in 1998, she says that although "it is clear that some genuinely damaging espionage did take place," the "government's evidence against the Rosenbergs was not overwhelming." (*Many Are the Crimes: McCarthyism in America.* Princeton, NJ: Princeton University Press, 1998, 179, 178)

p. 56, par. 1, For further information on McCarthyism, *see* Davis and Lunger, 95; Schrecker, 3–415; and Snowman, 121–124.

p. 58, par. 1, For more information on treatments for mental illness, *see* Maureen Empfield and Nicholas Bakalar, *Understanding Teenage Depression* (New York: Henry Holt and Company, 2001), 117–212; Frederick K. Goodwin and Kay Redfield Jamison, *Manic-Depressive Illness* (New York: Oxford University Press, 1990); and Martin L. Gross, *The Psychological Society* (New York: Random House, 1978), 142–246.

p. 61, par. 1, For additional information on American life in the late 1940s, the 1950s, and the early 1960s, *see* Davis and Lunger, 23–25, 67–68, 128–129, 149–154; Freidel, 461–572; and Snowman, 103–163.

Chapter 3
All references to the novel are to this edition: *The Bell Jar* (Foreword by Frances McCullough. New York: HarperCollins, 1996).

p. 66, par. 1, Many critics regard *The Bell Jar* as a coming-of-age novel of an American girl and compare it to young men's coming-of-age novels, particularly Salinger's *The Catcher in the Rye*. Tracy Brain says that "the American girl is *The Bell Jar*'s topic" (*The Other Sylvia Plath*. New York: Longman, 2001, 63), while Michael Davidson describes the novel as a "rite of passage from adolescence into womanhood" (*Guys Like Us: Citing Masculinity in Cold War Poetics*. Chicago: University of Chicago Press, 2004, 186). *See* also Linda Wagner-Martin, The Bell Jar: *A Novel of the Fifties* (New York: Twayne Publishers, 1992), 35–46.

p. 68, par. 1, Marjorie G. Perloff has an excellent discussion on the use of masks. *See* "'A Ritual for Being Born Twice': Sylvia Plath's *The Bell Jar*," *Contemporary Literature* 13.4 (Autumn 1972), 507–522.

p. 75, par. 1, For more information on the structure of the novel, *see* Eileen M. Aird, *Sylvia Plath* (Edinburgh, Scotland: Oliver and Boyd, 1973), 88–93; and Vance Bourjaily, "Victoria Lucas and Elly Higginbottom," in *Ariel Ascending: Writings about Sylvia Plath*, ed. Paul Alexander (New York: Harper & Row, 1985), 135–138.

p. 82, par. 2, For more information on Plath's use of electricity, *see* Bourjaily, 139–141.

p. 84, par. 2, The use of mirrors is discussed in Bourjaily, 141–142; and Perloff, 510–511.

p. 86, par. 3, The quotes in this paragraph are found in these sources:
"clever first novel": Robert Taubman, "Anti-heroes," *New Statesman* (January 25, 1963), 127–128, quoted in Wagner-Martin, The Bell Jar: *A Novel of the Fifties*, 10.
"a brilliant and moving book": Lawrence Lerner, "New Novels," *Listener* (January 31, 1963), 215, quoted in Wagner-Martin, The Bell Jar: *A Novel of the Fifties*, 11.
"astonishingly skillful": Rupert Butler, "New American Fiction: Three Disappointing Novels—but One Good One," *Time and Tide* (January 31, 1963), 34, quoted in Wagner-Martin, The Bell Jar: *A Novel of the Fifties*, 11.
"can certainly write": *Times Literary Supplement*, quoted in Lois Ames, "*The Bell Jar* and the Life of Sylvia Plath: A Biographical Note by Lois Ames." *The Bell Jar*, by Sylvia Plath (New York: HarperCollins, 1996), 13.

p. 87, par. 1, C. B. Cox. *Critical Quarterly* (1966); quoted in Wagner-Martin, The Bell Jar: *A Novel of the Fifties*, 11.

p. 87, par. 2, The quotes in this paragraph are found in these sources:
"it is impossible to read": Christopher Lehmann-Haupt, "An American Edition—At Last," *New York Times* (April 16, 1971), 35.
"wit and agony": Helen Dudar, *New York Post*, quoted in Wagner-Martin, The Bell Jar: *A Novel of the Fifties*, 13.
"a fine novel, as bitter": Robert Scholes, "Esther Came Back Like a Retreaded Tire," in *Ariel Ascending: Writings About Sylvia Plath*, ed. Paul Alexander (New York: Harper & Row, 1985), 130.

Chapter 4
All quotations from the poems are found in Sylvia Plath, *The Collected Poems*, ed. Ted Hughes (London: Faber and

Faber, 1981; New York: Harper & Row, 1981. Reprinted. New York: Harper Perennial, 1992).

p. 97, par. 1, There are many critics who regard "The Colossus" as a confessional poem about Plath's relationship with her dead father. For example, Jon Rosenblatt writes that "Plath imagines that the Colossus . . . is her father's dead body now lying broken in pieces on a hillside" (68). (*Sylvia Plath: The Poetry of Initiation*. Chapel Hill: University of North Carolina Press, 1979.) Grace Shulman says that "'The Colossus' represents a turning point in her poems about the father" (174). ("Sylvia Plath and Yaddo," in *Ariel Ascending: Writings about Sylvia Plath*, ed. Paul Alexander. New York: Harper & Row, 1985, 165–177.) Caroline King Barnard Hall feels that the "reference here is probably not only to her father as the statue that 'I' despairs of patching but also to herself" and her previous nervous breakdown. (*Sylvia Plath, Revised*. New York: Twayne, 1998, 60.)

p. 102, par. 1, For more information on the two biblical Lazaruses, *see* Maureen Curley, "Plath's 'Lady Lazarus,'" *The Explicator*, 59.4 (Summer 2001), 213–214; and Hall, 109.

p. 104, par. 1, For more information on the four sets of images used to identify Lady Lazarus, see Rosenblatt, 38–39.

p. 105, par. 1, For a discussion of Plath's use of "The Love Song of J. Alfred Prufrock," *see* Christina Britzolakis, *Sylvia Plath and the Theatre of Mourning* (Oxford: Clarendon Press, 1999), 152–153.

p. 105, par. 2, Plath's poetic techniques used in "Lady Lazarus" are discussed in a number of works. *See* Eileen

M. Aird, *Sylvia Plath* (Edinburgh, Scotland: Oliver and Boyd, 1973), 82–84; Britzolakis, 151–153; and Rosenblatt, 39–43.

p. 108, par. 1, The reviews quoted from Kinzie were first printed in the following works:
"simply writes good poetry": A. Alvarez, "Review of *The Colossus*," *The Observer Weekend Review*, 8, 842 (December 18, 1960).
"an individual manner": John Wain, "Review of *The Colossus*," *The Spectator*, 206.6, 916 (January 13, 1961), 50.
too tricky with "wordage": Dom Moraes, "Review of *The Colossus*," *Time and Tide*, 41.46 (November 19, 1960), 1413.
"outlook is gloomy . . . she is exhilarating to read": Peter Dickinson, "Review of *The Colossus*," *Punch* 239.6, 273 (December 7, 1960), 829.

p. 108, par. 2, The reviews quoted from Kinzie were first printed in the following works:
"asks us to feel emotions": Dan Jaffe, "Review of *Ariel*," *Saturday Review*, 49.42 (October 15, 1966), 29.
difficulty "of separating her work from her psychology": Barbara Howes, "A Note on *Ariel*," *Massachusetts Review*, 8.1 (Winter 1967), 225–226.
"the personal tragedy somehow reinforces poetry": Douglas M. Davis, "Review of *Ariel*," *National Observer*, 6.6 (February 6, 1967), 31.

p. 110, par. 3, For a discussion of Plath's poetry as confessional and feminist works, *see* Hall, 124–129.

Further Information

Further Reading

Becker, Jillian. *Giving Up: The Last Days of Sylvia Plath*. New York: St. Martin's Press, 2002.

Britzolakis, Christina. *Sylvia Plath and the Theatre of Mourning*. Oxford: Clarendon Press, 2001.

Bundtzen, Lynda K. *The Other Ariel*. Amherst: University of Massachusetts Press, 2001.

Kendall, Tim. *Sylvia Plath: A Critical Study*. London: Faber and Faber, 2001.

Middlebrook, Diane. *Her Husband: Hughes and Plath— A Marriage*. New York: Viking Press, 2003.

Wagner-Martin, Linda W. *Sylvia Plath—A Literary Life*. 2nd ed., New York: Palgrave, 2003.

Web Sites

http://www.poets.org
Includes biographical information, transcriptions of several poems, bibliography, and links.

http://www.sylviaplathforum.com
A message-board community to discuss Sylvia Plath's writings, life, and books about her.

Bibliography

Books by Sylvia Plath

Ariel. New York: Harper & Row, 1966.

Ariel: The Restored Edition. Foreword by Frieda Hughes. New York: HarperCollins, 2004.

The Bell Jar. New York: Harper & Row, 1971. Reprinted with foreword by Frances McCullough. New York: HarperCollins, 1996.

The Collected Poems. Edited by Ted Hughes. New York: HarperPerennial, 1992.

The Colossus and Other Poems. London: Faber and Faber, 1976.

The Journals of Sylvia Plath. Edited by Ted Hughes and Frances McCullough. New York: Dial Press, 1982.

Letters Home. Edited by Aurelia Schober Plath. New York: Harper & Row, 1975.

The Unabridged Journals of Sylvia Plath: 1950–1962. Edited by Karen V. Kukil. New York: Anchor Books, 2000.

Secondary Sources

Aird, Eileen M. *Sylvia Plath.* Edinburgh, Scotland: Oliver and Boyd, 1973.

Alexander, Paul, ed. *Ariel Ascending: Writings about Sylvia Plath.* New York: Harper & Row, 1984.

————. *Rough Magic: A Biography of Sylvia Plath*. Cambridge, MA: Da Capo Press, 1999.

Alvarez, A. *The Savage God: A Study of Suicide*. New York: Random House, 1971.

Ames, Lois. "*The Bell Jar* and the Life of Sylvia Plath: A Biographical Note by Lois Ames." In Plath, *The Bell Jar*, 3–15.

Axelrod, Steven Gould. "The Mirror and the Shadow: Plath's Poetics of Self-Doubt." *Contemporary Literature* 26.3 (Autumn 1985), 286–301.

Baldwin, Kate A. "The Radical Imaginary of *The Bell Jar*." *Novel: A Forum on Fiction* 38.1 (Fall 2004), 21–40.

Becker, Jillian. *Giving Up: The Last Days of Sylvia Plath*. New York: St. Martin's Press, 2002.

Berger, Philip A. "Shock Treatment." *The World Book Encyclopedia*. Chicago: World Book, 1986.

Bourjaily, Vance. "Victoria Lucas and Elly Higginbottom." In Alexander, *Ariel Ascending*, 134–151.

Boyer, Marilyn. "The Disabled Female Body as a Metaphor for Language in Sylvia Plath's *The Bell Jar*." *Women's Studies* 33.2 (March/April 2004), 199–223.

Brain, Tracy. *The Other Sylvia Plath*. New York: Longman, 2001.

Breslin, Paul. "Demythologizing Sylvia Plath." *Modernism/Modernity* 8.4 (2001), 675–679.

Britzolakis, Christina. *Sylvia Plath and the Theatre of Mourning*. Oxford: Clarendon Press, 1999.

Broe, Mary L. *Protean Poetic: The Poetry of Sylvia Plath.* Columbia: University of Missouri Press, 1980.

Bronfen, Elisabeth. *Sylvia Plath* (Writers and Their Work). Plymouth, UK: Northcote, 1998.

Brownstone, Alan. "Awesome Fragments." In Wagner, *Critical Essays on Sylvia Plath*, 55–56.

Bundtzen, Lynda L. *Plath's Incantations: Women and the Creative Process.* Ann Arbor: University of Michigan Press, 1983.

Butscher, Edward. *Sylvia Plath: Method and Madness.* New York: Seabury Press, 1976.

Collier, Peter, and David Horowitz. *The Kennedys: An American Drama.* New York: Summit Books, 1984.

Curley, Maureen. "Plath's 'Lady Lazarus.'" *The Explicator* 59.4 (Summer 2001), 213–214.

Davidson, Michael. *Guys Like Us: Citing Masculinity in Cold War Poetics.* Chicago: University of Chicago Press, 2004.

Davis, Daniel F., and Norman Lunger. *A History of the United States Since 1945.* New York: Scholastic, 1987.

Dulles, Foster Rhea. *Twentieth Century America.* Boston: Houghton Mifflin, 1945.

Dumond, Dwight Lowell. *America in Our Time: 1896–1946.* New York: Henry Holt and Company, 1947.

Eliot, T. S. "The Love Song of J. Alfred Prufrock." In *The Norton Anthology of English Literature.* Vol 2. Edited by Stephen Greenblatt. 8th ed. New York: W. W. Norton, 2006, 2289–2293.

Empfield, Maureen, and Nicholas Bakalar. *Understanding Teenage Depression: A Guide to Diagnosis, Treatment, and Management.* New York: Henry Holt and Company, 2001.

Epstein, Cynthia Fuchs. "Woman." *The World Book Encyclopedia.* Chicago: World Book, 1986, 316–322.

Friedan, Betty. *Feminine Mystique.* New York: Norton, 1963.

Freidel, Frank. *America in the Twentieth Century.* New York: Alfred A. Knopf, 1960.

Grant, Damian. *"Winter Trees."* In Wagner, *Critical Essays on Sylvia Plath,* 53–55.

Hall, Caroline King Barnard. *Sylvia Plath, Revised.* New York: Twayne Publishers, 1998.

Harris, Mason. *"The Bell Jar." West Coast Review* (October 1973), 54–56.

Hayman, Ronald. *The Death and Life of Sylvia Plath.* Secaucus, NJ: Carol Publishing Group, 1991.

Hughes, Merritt Y. "Notes." In Milton, *Paradise Lost.*

Hughes, Ted. "Notes on the Chronological Order of Sylvia Plath's Poems." In Newman, *The Art of Sylvia Plath,* 187–195.

———. "Notes on Poems 1956–1963." In Plath, *The Collected Poems,* 275–296.

Jamison, Kay Redfield. *Touched with Fire: Manic-Depressive Illness and the Artistic Temperament.* New York: Free Press, 1993.

Jerome, Judson. *The Poet's Handbook.* Cincinnati: Writer's Digest Books, 1980.

Jones, A. R. "On 'Daddy.'" In Newman, *The Art of Sylvia Plath*, 230–236.

Kendall, Tim. *Sylvia Plath: A Critical Study*. London: Faber & Faber, 2001.

Kinzie, Mary. "An Informal Check List of Criticism." In Newman, *The Art of Sylvia Plath*, 283–304.

Kroll, Judith. *Chapters in a Mythology: The Poetry of Sylvia Plath*. New York: Harper, 1976.

Laing, R. D. *The Divided Self*. Baltimore, MD: Penguin, 1960 and 1970.

Lant, Kathleen Margaret. "The Big Strip Tease: Female Bodies and Male Power in the Poetry of Sylvia Plath." *Contemporary Literature* 34.4 (Winter 1993), 620–669.

Lehmann-Haupt, Christopher. "An American Edition—At Last." *New York Times*, April 16, 1971, 35.

Lerner, Laurence. "Sylvia Plath." In Wagner, *Critical Essays on Sylvia Plath*, 64–67.

Lindberg-Seyersted, Brita. "Sylvia Plath's Psychic Landscapes." *English Studies* 71.6 (December 1990), 509–522.

Markey, Janice. *A Journey in the Red Eye: The Poetry of Sylvia Plath: A Critique*. London: Women's, 1993.

McCullough, Frances. Foreword to *The Bell Jar*. In Plath, *The Bell Jar*, ix–xvii.

Metzger, Bruce M., and Roland E. Murphy, eds. *The New Oxford Annotated Bible with the Apocrypha: An Ecumenical Study Bible*. New York: Oxford University Press, 1994.

Middlebrook, Diane. *Her Husband: Hughes and Plath—A Marriage*. New York: Viking Press, 2003.

Milton, John. *Paradise Lost*. Edited by Merritt Y. Hughes. New York: Odyssey Press, 1935.

Moers, Ellen. *Literary Women*. Garden City, NY: Doubleday, 1976.

Moss, Howard. "Dying: An Introduction." In Alexander, *Ariel Ascending*, 125–129.

Myers, E. Lucas. "The Tranquilized Fifties." In Wagner, *Critical Essays on Sylvia Plath*, 30–32.

Nance, Guinevara A., and Judith P. Jones. "Doing Away with Daddy: Exorcism and Sympathetic Magic in Plath's Poetry." In Wagner, *Critical Essays on Sylvia Plath*, 124–130.

Narbeshuber, Lisa. "The Poetics of Torture: The Spectacle of Sylvia Plath's Poetry." *Canadian Review of American Studies* 34.2 (2004), 185–203.

Newman, Charles, ed. *The Art of Sylvia Plath, A Symposium*. Bloomington: Indiana University Press, 1970.

Nims, John Frederick. "The Poetry of Sylvia Plath: A Technical Analysis." In Newman, *The Art of Sylvia Plath*, 136–152.

Perloff, Marjorie G. "'A Ritual for Being Born Twice': Sylvia Plath's *The Bell Jar*." *Contemporary Literature* 13.4 (Autumn 1972), 507–522.

Plumly, Stanley. "What Ceremony of Words." In Alexander, *Ariel Ascending*, 13–25.

Pollitt, Katha. "A Note of Triumph." In Wagner, *Critical Essays on Sylvia Plath*, 67–72.

Porter, Peter. "Collecting Her Strength." In Wagner, *Critical Essays on Sylvia Plath*, 46–47.

Pritchard, William H. "An Interesting Minor Poet?" In Wagner, *Critical Essays on Sylvia Plath*, 72–77.

Rose, Jacqueline. *The Haunting of Sylvia Plath*. Cambridge: Harvard University Press, 1992.

Rosenblatt, Jon. *Sylvia Plath: The Poetry of Initiation*. Chapel Hill: University of North Carolina Press, 1979.

Rosenthal, M. L. "Sylvia Plath and Confessional Poetry." In Newman, *The Art of Sylvia Plath*, 69–76.

Scholes, Robert . "Esther Came Back Like a Retreaded Tire." In Alexander, *Ariel Ascending*, 130–133.

Schrecker, Ellen. *Many Are the Crimes: McCarthyism in America*. Princeton, NJ: Princeton University Press, 1998.

Schulman, Grace. "Sylvia Plath and Yaddo." In Alexander *Ariel Ascending*, 165–177.

Shakespeare, William. *The Tempest. The Complete Works of Shakespeare*, edited by David Bevington. Updated 4th ed. New York: Longman, 1997, 1526–1558.

Snowman, Daniel. *America Since 1920*. New York: Harper & Row, 1968.

Steiner, Nancy Hunter. *A Closer Look at Ariel: A Memory of Sylvia Plath*. New York: Popular Library, 1973.

Stevenson, Anne. *Bitter Fame: A Life of Sylvia Plath*. Boston: Houghton Mifflin, 1989.

Tanner, Tony. *City of Words: American Fiction, 1950–1970*. New York: Harper & Row, 1971.

Thompson, Catherine. "'Dawn Poems in Blood': Sylvia Plath and PMS." *Tri–Quarterly* 80 (Winter 1990–1991), 221–249.

Uroff, Margaret Dickie. *Sylvia Plath and Ted Hughes*. Urbana: University of Illinois Press, 1979.

Van Dyne, Susan R. *Revising Life: Sylvia Plath's Ariel Poems*. Chapel Hill: University of North Carolina Press, 1993.

Vendler, Helen. "An Intractable Metal." In Alexander, *Ariel Ascending: Writings About Sylvia Plath*, 1–12.

Wagner, Linda W., ed. *Critical Essays on Sylvia Plath*. Boston: G. K. Hall, 1984.

————. "Introduction." In Wagner, *Critical Essays on Sylvia Plath*, 1–24.

Wagner–Martin, Linda W. The Bell Jar: *A Novel of the Fifties*. New York: Twayne, 1992.

————. *Sylvia Plath: A Biography*. New York: St. Martin's Press, 1987.

West, Paul. "*Crossing the Water*." In Wagner, *Critical Essays on Sylvia Plath*, 48–51.

Whitehead, Barbara Dafoe. "Plight of the High-Status Woman." *Atlantic Monthly* 284.6 (December 1999), 120, 122–124.

Yalom, Marilyn. *Maternity, Mortality, and the Literature of Madness*. University Park: Pennsylvania State University Press, 1985.

Index

Page numbers in **boldface** are illustrations, tables, and charts.
Proper names of fictional characters are shown by (C).

About Sylvia/Poems by Diane Ackerman, 116
Ackerman, Diane, 116
Adams, Ryan, 118
alliteration, 95
Alvarez, A., 37, 47, 87–88, 114
American complacency, 57, 58–59
American domestic life, 57, 59–61, 70, 79, 87–89
antihero, 61
"Ariel," 92–96, 110, 118
Ariel, 7, 12, 42–44, 86–87, **90**, 91, 108–109, 113–114
Ariel: The Restored Edition, **90**, 91, 109–110, 114–115
assonance, 95

Baldwin, James, 61
Becker, Jillian, 41, 44–48, 115
beekeeping, 12, 40, 42
The Bell Jar, 7, 16, **18**, 23, 37, 41–43, 51, 55, 61, **62**, 63–89, 94, 113–114, 116, 118
  analysis, 74–86
  characters, 75–78, 115
  literary reception, 86–89
  motifs, 84–86
  narrative voice, 75
  plot, 63–66
  structure, 74–75
  symbols, 78–84, **79, 80**
  themes and issues, 66–74
bell jar as symbol, 78–79
Betsy (C), 63–64, 68, 76, 85
bipolar illness, 26
Birthday Letters, 116

Cal (C), 78
Cee, Jay (C), 64, 68–69, 70
Cold War, 54
The Collected Poems, 7, 91, 109, 114
The Collected Poems: The Journals of Sylvia Plath, 114
colloquial language, use of, 105
"The Colossus," 92, 96–97
The Colossus, 7, 12, 36–37, 39, 91, 108, 113
communism, 54–57, **56**
Compton, Elizabeth, 40–41
"confessional poetry," 108–109, 110, 115–116
Constantin (C), 64, 69–70, 78, 81
Conway, Dodo (C), 68
Crossing the Water, 91, 109, 114
Cuban missile crisis, 57

"Daddy," 92, 97–101, 110
Dalton, Katharina, 50
death motifs, 85–86
Dee Dee (C), 70
depression, 21–23, 25–27, 32, 34, 41, 43–44, 58, **62**, 87–88
  depicted in *The Bell Jar*, 64, 74, 75
  as suicide reason, 47–50
devil/vampire images, 100
diabetes, 14, 15
Doctor Gordon (C), 65, 69–70, 73–74, 82
Doctor Nolan (C), 65, 69, 72, 76, 82

Doreen (C), 63–64, 68, 70, 74, 76, 83, 85
drug therapy, 44, 49–51, 57–58

Eisenhower, Dwight D., 55, 88
electricity symbol, 81–82
Eliot, T. S., 105
essay collections, 116

fame, desire for, 27, 37, 39, 47
fig tree symbol, 79, **79**, 81
free verse, 97
Freud, Sigmund, 58
Friedan, Betty, 60, 89
Fulbright fellowship, **28**, 29, 31

Gilling, Joan (C), 65, 70, 73–77, 85, 86
Goldemberg, Rose Leiman, 118
Great Depression, 53
Greenwood, Esther (C), **18**, 63–65, 74–78, 94
  Esther/Elly, 63, 68, 74
  illness/death motifs, 84–86
  inferior position of women theme, 71–73, 89
  medical care quality theme, 73–74
  search for identity theme, 66–70, **67**
  use of symbolism, 78–79, 81–84
Guinea, Philomena (C), 65, 69, 70

Higginbottom, Elly (C), 63, 68, 74
Hitler, Adolf, **52**, 53, 54, 100
Horder, John, 45, 49
Hughes, Frieda Rebecca, 37–38, **38**, **90**
Hughes, Nicholas Farrar, **38**, 39
Hughes, Shura, 45

Hughes, Ted, 7, 30–34, **30**, 36–38, 44–45, 50–51, 115–116
  adultery, 39–42, 43, 47–49
  as executor, **90**, 91–92, 98, 101, 113

iambic meter, 92, 97
illness motifs, 84–85
inferior position of women theme, 70–73, 89
internal rhyme, 95, 105
Irwin (C), 65, 70, 78
Isaiah, 94

Jeff, Christine, 118
Jody (C), 70
John, Gospel of, 102–103
Johnny Panic and the Bible of Dreams, 114
Jong, Erica, 116

Kennedy, John F., 57, 58
Korean War, 54–55
Kübler-Ross, Elisabeth, 87

"Lady Lazarus," 92, 101–107, 110, 118
Langridge, Charles, 45
Lazarus, biblical, 102–105, **102**
Letters Home, 114, **117**, 118
Lowell, Robert, 38
Lucas, Victoria, 7, 43, 86
Luke, Gospel of, 103

Mademoiselle magazine, **18**, 19, 23, **24**, 25
manic-depressive illness, 26
Mao Zedong, 54
Marco (C), 64, 68–69, 74, 78, 83
McCarthy, Joseph, 55, 56, **56**
McCullough, Frances, 43, 87, 118
medical care quality theme, 73–74

mental illness, 87–88, 96, 108
  depicted in *The Bell Jar*, 65,
  74–75, 77, 83, 85
  treatment for, 26–27, 57–58,
  59, 65, 73–75, 82
metaphor, use of, 91, 107
"Metaphors," 92, 107
Milton, John, 93
mirrors as symbols, 83–84
Mr. Manzi (C), 66
Mrs. Greenwood (C), 68, 77
Mrs. Willard (C), 68, 72, 77, 94

narrative voice, 75
Nazis, **52**, 53–54, 97,
  99–100, 104–105, 116
Norris, Myra, 44–45
Norton, Dick, 20–21

off rhyme, 91, 105
"The Other," 40

Paltrow, Gwyneth, **112**, 118
patriarchal society, 7, 12, 21,
  34, 7, 60–61, 99–100, 115
Pearl Harbor, 53
physical illness theme, 84–85
Plath, Aurelia Schober, 10–12,
  11, 14–15, 19, 26–27, 34, 36,
  40–42, 45, 48, **117**
Plath, Otto Emil, 10–12, **11**,
  14–15, 27
Plath, Sylvia
  childhood, 10–15, **11**, **13**,
  53–54
  college, 17–32, 54, 57
  as cult figure, 113, 114
  disillusionment, 21, 60–61, 64
  early influences, 12–13, **13**
  early publication, 7, 15–16,
  18, 23, 31, 114
  final days, 43–45, **46**
  gravestone, **46**, 115
  literary criticism of, 107–111

marriage, 9, 29–39, 40–43, \48
mental illness, 7, 17, 20–23,
  26, 28, 50, 83, 96, 106. *See*
  also depression.
as perfectionist, 17, 19, 26, 42
physical illness, 7, 15, 20–21,
  37, 42–43, 45–46, 49
plays, 39, 91
poetry, 12, 14, 33, 91–111
  in popular culture, **112**, 118
prose, 7, 63–89, 116
rhyming method, 91–92, 95,
  97, 101, 105
status as major writer, 116
suicide, 7–9, **8**, 17, 23, 26, **35**,
  44–51, 86–87, 98,
  114–115
as teacher, 32–33
temperament, 16, 20, 22–23,
  28–29, 49
as victimized, 7, 42–43, 47,
  60–61, 86, 98–99, 113, 115
voice, 7, 75, 110–111, 118
Plath, Warren Joseph, 12, **13**, 45
Plumly, Stanley, 96
Pope, Alexander, 93
popular culture, **112**, 118
premenstrual syndrome (PMS),
  22, 50
Prouty, Olive Higgins, 17, 26–27
psychoanalysis, 27, 57, 58
  depicted in *The Bell Jar*, 65, 75
psychosurgery (lobotomy),
  57–58, 73, 76
Pulitzer Prize in Poetry, 7, 109, 114

repetition, use of, 105
Rosenberg, Julius and Ethel,
  55, 63, **80**, 82–83

Salinger, J. D., 61, 86, 87
Salk, Jonas, 57
Saxton Fellowship, 39
schizophrenia, 26, 58, 88
search for identity theme,
  66–70, **67**

secretarial skills, 26, 32, 33,
68, 71, 77
Segal, Erich, 87
Seventeen magazine, 8, 16, 19
Sexton, Anne, 35, **35**, 116
Shakespeare, William, 93
Shepard, Alan B. Jr., 57
Shepherd, Lenny (C), 63, 69,
74, 78, 83
shock therapy, 26–27, 57–58, **59**
depicted in *The Bell Jar*,
65, 73–75, 82
slant rhyme, 91, 95, 105
stanza form, 92, 95, 97, 105
Starbuck, George, 35
Steinbeck, John, 53
Steinem, Gloria, 60, **61**
Steiner, Nancy Hunter,
19–20, 27, 28–29, 47
Stevenson, Adlai, 60
suicide, 7–9, 8, 17, 23, 26, **35**,
44–45, 86–87, 114–115
depicted in *The Bell Jar*, 65,
73–75, 77, 83–84
depicted in poetry, 98, 101,
104, 108
reasons for, 45, 47–51

Sylvia (film), **112**, 118
terza rima stanzas, 92, 95, 105
Thomas, Dylan, **24**, 25, 31
Three Women (play), 39, 91

*The Unabridged Journals of
Sylvia Plath*, 114–115

Valerie (C), 73–74, 76
victim/victimization theme,
98–101, 106, 110
Vietnam War, 57

Winter Trees, 91, 114
women, traditional role of, 12,
21, 34, 37, 59–60, **61**, 88–89,
115
in *The Bell Jar*, 63, 66–73,
67, 75, 77, 79, 81, 85,
88–89
in poetry, 99–100, 106, 110
women's rights movement,
60–61, **61**, 70, 87, 88, 89
World War II, **52**, 53, 54, 57
writer's block, 33, 36

About the Author

RAYCHEL HAUGRUD REIFF, a professor of English at the University of Wisconsin–Superior, has published fifteen articles on literary topics and effective teaching techniques in various journals and books. Her most recent book in Marshall Cavendish Benchmark's Writers and Their Works series is *Edgar Allan Poe: Tales and Poems*. She lives in Superior, Wisconsin.